T0328582

Cambridge Elements ≡

Elements in Islam and the Sciences
edited by
Nidhal Guessoum
American University of Sharjah, United Arab Emirates
Stefano Bigliardi
Al Akhawayn University in Ifrane, Morocco

ISLAM AND SCIENCE

Past, Present, and Future Debates

Nidhal Guessoum
*American University of Sharjah,
United Arab Emirates*

Stefano Bigliardi
Al Akhawayn University in Ifrane, Morocco

CAMBRIDGE
UNIVERSITY PRESS

Shaftesbury Road, Cambridge CB2 8EA, United Kingdom

One Liberty Plaza, 20th Floor, New York, NY 10006, USA

477 Williamstown Road, Port Melbourne, VIC 3207, Australia

314–321, 3rd Floor, Plot 3, Splendor Forum, Jasola District Centre,
New Delhi – 110025, India

103 Penang Road, #05–06/07, Visioncrest Commercial, Singapore 238467

Cambridge University Press is part of Cambridge University Press & Assessment,
a department of the University of Cambridge.

We share the University's mission to contribute to society through the pursuit of
education, learning and research at the highest international levels of excellence.

www.cambridge.org
Information on this title: www.cambridge.org/9781009266512

DOI: 10.1017/9781009266550

First published 2023

A catalogue record for this publication is available from the British Library.

ISBN 978-1-009-26651-2 Paperback
ISSN 2754-7094 (online)
ISSN 2754-7086 (print)

Islam and Science

Past, Present, and Future Debates

Elements in Islam and the Sciences

DOI: 10.1017/9781009266550
First published online: March 2023

Nidhal Guessoum
American University of Sharjah, United Arab Emirates

Stefano Bigliardi
Al Akhawayn University in Ifrane, Morocco

Author for correspondence: Nidhal Guessoum, nguessoum@aus.edu

Abstract: This first Element in the series *Islam and the Sciences* is introductory and aims to give readers a general overview of the wide and rich scope of interactions of Islam with the sciences, including past disputes, current challenges, and future outlooks. The Element introduces the main voices and schools of thought, adopting a historical approach to show the evolution of the debates: Khan's naturalism, Al-Jisr's hermeneutics, Abduh's modernist Islam, Nasr's perennialist and sacred science, Al-Attas Islamic science, Sardar and the *Ijmalis'* ethical science, Al-Faruqi's Islamization of knowledge, Bucaille's and El-Naggar's "miraculous scientific content in the Qur'an," Abdus Salam's universal science, Hoodbhoy's and Edis's secularism, and the harmonization of the "new generation." The Element also maps out new and emerging topics that are beginning to reignite the debates, before a concluding section examines how issues of Islam and science are playing out in the media, in public discourse, and in education.

This Element also has a video abstract: www.cambridge.org/islamandscience

Keywords: Islam and science, Islam and evolution, religion and science, Qur'an and science, pedagogy of Islam and science

ISBNs: 9781009266512 (PB), 9781009266550 (OC)
ISSNs: 2754-7094 (online), 2754-7086 (print)

Contents

Foreword

In the spring of 2017, a scandal in Tunisia shook the Arab scientific and educational world: A doctoral student submitted a thesis in environmental science arguing "scientifically" (but freely mixing in large doses of religious ideas) that the Earth is flat, motionless, and relatively young (only 13,500 years old). She also claimed that the Earth is the center of the universe, and even more daringly, explicitly rejected the physics of Newton and Einstein, the astronomy of Copernicus and Kepler (claiming to see "weaknesses in their foundations"), big bang cosmology, and most of modern geology and climatology.

The student submitted her thesis after five years of work; it was then sent to two reviewers, passing the first stage of approvals. Assessors' reports were expected soon after, for the thesis defense to be scheduled. At this stage, fate happily intervened: A copy of the thesis was "leaked" to the former president of the Tunisian Astronomical Society, who, after verifying that it was not a hoax, sounded the alarm by posting the general conclusions of the thesis on Facebook. The news reverberated around the world for weeks . . .

This shocking example does not represent the entire realm of Islam and science today, and one can cite much more positive developments. For instance, stem-cell research is thriving in the Arab-Muslim world, including in Saudi Arabia and Iran, and this required *fatwa*s (religious rulings) to be issued. Likewise, the Arab-Muslim world is witnessing a space-age boom: from Malaysia, which sent an astronaut to space in 2007 (and to that end organized a two-day conference to discuss how the astronaut would perform prayers and other Islamic duties in space), to the UAE, which sent an astronaut up to the International Space Station in 2019 and a probe to Mars in 2020, the latter arriving without any problems and going into orbit around the red planet in February 2021.

The examples above, and many more that one could mention from the Muslim world, show that relating Islam and science is far from simple and requires some careful and rigorous analyses, which is one of the main objectives of this Element.

This is the first Element in the series *Elements in Islam and the Sciences*. It aims to introduce the reader to the wide, rich, and complex interaction of Islam with the sciences, past and present, at multiple levels and on various topics, including current views and debates and future outlooks.

The Element introduces the main voices and schools of thought in this field adopting a historical approach, from medieval times to the twenty-first century. A spectrum of positions are summarized and reviewed, from Ash'arism and Mu'tazilism (the debates on causality) to naturalism and modernism (Sayyid Ahmad Khan and Muhammad Abduh), traditionalism and perennialism (Seyyed Hossein Nasr), the Islamization of knowledge (Ismail Raji Al-Faruqi), Islamic science (Syed Muhammad Naquib Al-Attas), *i'jaz 'ilmi* (scientific content in the Qur'an – Maurice Bucaille and Zaghloul El-Naggar), secularism (Pervez Hoodbhoy and Taner Edis), and more.

Last but not least, this Element devotes a full section to new and future debates in Islam and science, including those concerning consciousness, free will, randomness, artificial intelligence, and transhumanism, not to mention old/new topics such as surrogacy and transsexual issues, all of which are covered with the goal of inviting novel explorations and propositions.

1 Science, Religion/Islam, and How They Relate

Discussions of the relation between science and religion, or between reason and faith, well predate the development of modern science. Ever since humans started to develop a rational methodology for finding "truths" and ascertaining their validity, that is, since the appearance of (systematic) philosophy, the question of the relation between that kind of knowledge and what religions and their revelations teach became a central one in humans' quest for understanding.

Let's start by defining both "religion" and "science" – in fact we may need to also define "Islam," as different people and even scholars have varying understandings of it – before we examine the relations that they may have.

Religion and Islam

Religion, in general, is a system of beliefs ("dogmas"), practices (or "rituals"), and/or norms (or "rules") of behavior. Religion is usually based on faith, in God, Spirit (divine), "spirits" (nonmaterial beings), "spirit" (a nonphysical dimension of humans), prophets, saints, sacred texts, spiritual or mystical experience, reincarnation, and other ideas of this kind. While not all of these concepts are carried by all religions, it is important to note that all are nonnatural/nonphysical, hence outside of the realm of natural science, as we shall define it. However, they may well be the subject of fields such as psychology, anthropology, and other social sciences.

Islam is one of the "monotheistic" religions, that is, it starts with the strong belief in the One God, Allah. Indeed, this "unicity," known in Islamic vocabulary as *tawhid*, is by far the most important concept in Islam. Relations with God, through prayer, inspiration, and (for prophets) revelation, are a central idea; in fact, being (constantly) mindful of God (*taqwa*) is supposed to be the guiding principle for humans. Additional essential beliefs in Islam are stated in one famous *hadith*:[1] belief in prophets (humans who receive divine revelation),

---

[1] A *hadith* is a statement, an action, or an acquiescence (something witnessed and not criticized or warned against) by Prophet Muhammad, as reported by his companions. Scholars, for example Bukhari, Muslim, Tirmidhi, and others (a century or more after the death of the Prophet),

sacred (divinely revealed) texts, the Day of Judgment, angels (who transmit the revelation or perform tasks as instructed by God), and "fate."[2]

Islam is also often characterized by its famous "five pillars": the belief in Allah and Muhammad as His (final) messenger, the five daily prayers, giving alms (obligatory charity on one's financial and material property), the fasting in Ramadan, and the pilgrimage (*hajj*), which should be undertaken at least once in a lifetime by those who can afford it. Except for the first pillar, which is a belief, all others are practices and rituals. Finally, Islamic norms of behavior or ethics are summed up in the last part of the same *hadith* that defined the six essential beliefs and the five pillars: to "worship God as if you see Him, for if you do not see Him, He certainly sees you"; that is, one should be constantly mindful of God (*taqwa*) and behave accordingly.

Islam's holy book, the Qur'an, is absolutely central. As Massimo Campanini stated, "Islam is a culture grounded on a book, the Qur'an" (Campanini 2005: 48). Other scholars have noted the Qur'an's central place in Islam. Fr. Georges C. Anawati, Egyptian Dominican friar and specialist of Islamic thought, wrote: "In the beginning was the Qur'an" (Anawati 1979: 358). Many have stressed the key role that the Qur'an plays in Muslims' lives; Suha Taji-Farouki notes that "millions of people refer to the Qur'an daily to justify their aspirations or to explain their actions," adding that the scale of this kind of reference has in contemporary times reached "unprecedented [levels] in the Islamic experience" (Taji-Farouki 2004: 20). The Qur'an plays a central role in defining not just the beliefs and the behavior of Muslims, but their worldview as well. Kenneth Cragg notes that Muslims regard it as "the ground plan of all knowledge" (Cragg 1998: 15); he adds: "We may say that if Muslims are to be assured on any and every issue, they will need to be Qur'anically persuaded, however variously they invoke it" (Cragg 1998: 28).

Science

Before we can properly define "science," we need to distinguish it from "knowledge"; "knowledge" also needs to be distinguished from "information," which itself needs to be distinguished from "data."

- Data is raw numbers, texts, figures, symbols, and so on, which on their own have no meaning.
- Information is data that has been structured or placed in context.

---

collected thousands of *hadith*s and rated them as "authentic," "fair," "weak," and so on, depending on the reliability of their narrators and the multiplicity of the chains of narration of a given *hadith*.

[2] *Qada' wa-qadar*, also translated and interpreted as "destiny," and sometimes labeled as "preordained," has been the source of substantial debates among Muslim scholars.

- Knowledge is information that has been treated into an actionable state: understanding something, relating to other, and so on.
- Science (natural or social) is a systematized body of knowledge, built on a methodology that seeks to reach objective results (facts and theories).

Since knowledge, as we shall see, is particularly important in the culture of Islam, we should look at it more closely and raise a few issues that will resurface later in our exploration. There are various sources of knowledge: traditional/ religious versus modern (evidence-based); personal versus collective; formal versus informal; explicit versus implicit; "common sense" or intuitive versus tested. Can the same data/facts lead to different knowledge for different people? Is scientific knowledge of a "special kind"? When does knowledge become "truth"? Is knowledge subject to authority?

Defining science is not straightforward. First, in the Islamic tradition, until it was introduced in Islamic lands in its new, "modern," or "Western" version (mostly in the nineteenth century by colonial powers), science was not distinguished from other forms of knowledge. It was all referred to as *'ilm*, a term which basically means "knowledge" and which plays a significant role in the culture of Islam. Furthermore, most of the Muslim scholars who wrote about natural phenomena, whether empirically, theoretically, or even speculatively, filed them under philosophy, alongside other fields such as ethics, political philosophy, metaphysics, and logic.

In the West also, for a long time "science" was referred to as "natural philosophy," that is, the study of natural phenomena, signifying that it was under the umbrella of philosophy (as it was in the East). The differentiation of science from philosophy and its splitting into branches (natural, social) came only in recent centuries. Likewise, "science" gingerly split from "philosophy" in the Islamic world at the hands of Al-Biruni and Ibn Al-Haytham (both in the eleventh century, but separately) and more fully with the scientific revolution in Europe (seventeenth century onward).

Current dictionaries offer multiple, more-or-less-similar definitions of "science":

- "The intellectual and practical activity encompassing the systematic study of the structure and behaviour of the physical and natural world through observation and experiment." (*New Oxford American Dictionary*)
- "(Knowledge from) the careful study of the structure and behaviour of the physical world, especially by watching, measuring, and doing experiments, and the development of theories to describe the results of these activities." (*Cambridge Dictionary*)

- "Knowledge or a system of knowledge covering general truths or the operation of general laws especially as obtained and tested through the scientific method; knowledge or a system of knowledge concerned with the physical world and its phenomena: NATURAL SCIENCE."[3] (*Merriam-Webster Dictionary*)

Countless books discuss the "philosophy of science," a discipline whose goal is to delineate science and characterize it, with the aim of ensuring rigor and awareness of whatever limitations it may carry. In *Philosophy of Science: A Very Short Introduction*, Samir Okasha starts by asking: "Surely science is just the attempt to understand, explain, and predict the world we live in?" (Okasha 2016: 1). While highlighting several important aspects of science, this first-draft definition may be lacking in some respects; most notably, it says nothing about the nature of the enterprise of constructing *objective* explanations.

Ziauddin Sardar (more on him later) provides a more precise definition: "[Science is] an organized, systematic and disciplined mode of inquiry based on experimentation and empiricism that produces repeatable and applicable results universally, across all cultures" (Sardar 2006b: 181). This definition has the virtue of emphasizing the goals of objectivity (repeatability, universality) and testability (experimentation, empiricism). It also implicitly restricts the field to the natural sciences.

The essential characteristic of science may very well consist in the method and process it has developed, almost canonized, and required everyone who practices science to adopt, with the aim of ensuring that we "do not fool ourselves," as Richard Feynman so eloquently phrased it. That is what we call "the scientific method" and what we uphold as the most glorious aspect of science, even more marvelous than the array of results that scientists have achieved.

However, some important aspects are still missing from the above description: (a) it downplays the personal/subjective elements; (b) it does not emphasize the role of the scientific community in the gathering of facts and the checking not only of results and predictions (experimental and theoretical) but also the internal consistency of any proposed theory/model. This second (peer-reviewing) aspect is in fact what has given science its robustness, allowing it to distinguish erroneous claims from true results. This part is often greatly underappreciated by the public at large, including highly educated but nonscientific groups.

The subjective human element in the scientific enterprise is its Achilles' heel. Few people, even in the scientific community, are fully aware of it. However, it is

---

[3] *New Oxford American Dictionary* (2010), eds A. Stevenson & C. A. Lindberg (3rd ed.; New York: Oxford University Press), p. 26,281; *Cambridge Dictionary* (2022), "Science," https://dictionary.cambridge.org/dictionary/english/science; Merriam-Webster Dictionary (2022), "Science," www.merriam-webster.com/dictionary/science.

often exaggerated by the detractors of science, including traditionalists, cultural relativists, and other postmodernists. For instance, philosopher William Chittick dismisses the claim that modern science carries any true objectivity, considering it simply as "a vast structure of beliefs and presuppositions" (Chittick 2007: 24). For him, "what people call 'science' is strikingly similar to what in [previous] times was called 'sorcery'. Certainly, the goal is exactly the same" (Chittick 2007: 34). This overly harsh description and assessment of science is probably based on an erroneous understanding of the scientific enterprise, along with its foundations, methods, analyses, results, and interpretations.

From the discussion in this section, we may summarily define (natural) science as the attempt to know the physical world, based on observations and experiments, both for our understanding (satisfying our curiosity) and for our benefit. Moreover, science is methodical, tries to be rigorous, and aims to be objective (independent of one's personality, background, beliefs, etc.). Science is also supposed to be evidence-based, falsifiable, and repeatable. After much work, it produces "facts" (e.g. the Earth is round and orbits the Sun) and "theories" (a box of facts, laws, models, and other pieces, which fit together and explain a number of phenomena and observations), but its results are often open to interpretation.

Relations between Religion/Islam and Science

Having defined and characterized religion and Islam as well as science and the kind of knowledge it provides, we can ask how they relate and interact. Do they somehow clash, particularly in the claims they make about humans, nature, phenomena (how they occur and what they mean), and God's role in it all? Are they two "magisteria," separate but complementary teachings, or fields of human thought, knowledge, and existence/experience?

Science and religion are two approaches to the world. Claiming to describe "reality" and explain our existence and that of the world, they often compete for the place of guiding principle in humans' minds. The famous physicist and mathematician Freeman Dyson described religion as "an essential part of the human condition, more deeply rooted and more widely shared than science" (Dyson 2007: 131). Science and religion are fundamentally different conceptual systems, however. It is thus of utmost importance to understand their differences, their domains of overlap, and the possible ways in which they can interact. The realization that there is much to discuss in this regard has given birth to the field now known as "science and religion." This encompasses two subdomains: (a) the academic arena, where issues about science and religion are rigorously discussed (journals, conferences, courses, theses, etc.); (b) a public arena, where a "free-for-all" exists through various media about many topics pertaining to science and religion.

This field, although recent, has explored a number of important issues of relevance to humanity in general and to specific cultures. One main idea that should be stressed is the basic but essential distinction between various types of knowledge (science, natural and social, humanities, religion, etc.). Another is what people must know and accept as true ("established knowledge") versus what they can choose to believe. Deeper into the subject, we find issues of general epistemology: What are valid modes of knowing? Is scientific knowledge (more) objective and universal? Is it constantly evolving or are some of its results definite and permanent? Does science provide a worldview or only factual information? How does scientific knowledge relate to (accept, reject, ignore) "revealed knowledge"? How is one to understand and interpret scriptural statements, stories, descriptions, and so on? Is it all interpretative, or are some religious statements more fixed in meaning? How does scientific knowledge affect scriptural exegesis?

As we have mentioned, because "science" was not originally distinguished from "knowledge" in Islamic culture, it did not have a separate word/term in Arabic and came to be referred to as *'ilm* – the same as "knowledge"; however, to stress the wider meaning of knowledge and to differentiate it from *'ilm*, some (modern) authors started to use *ma'rifa* for "knowledge," while *hikma*, literally meaning "wisdom," was often used to refer to philosophy. The decision to identify "science" as *'ilm* was made by Muslim reformers in the nineteenth and twentieth centuries partly to legitimize this "Western" science, which was seen as the crucial factor that had propelled European powers well ahead of the Muslim world.

'Ilm enjoys high esteem in the Islamic culture, including in the Qur'an. For instance, one reads: "Are those who know equal with those who know not?" (39:9), and "Truly fear Allah those among His Servants who have knowledge" (35:28). Indeed, the Qur'an encourages Muslims to explore and discover the world: "Say: Travel in the land and see how He originated creation" (29:20). One of the main contributors to the contemporary debate on Islam and science, Iranian physicist Mehdi Golshani, emphasizes that, "In the Holy Qur'an, the word *'ilm* (knowledge) and its derivatives are used more than 780 times" (Golshani 2003a: 65).

The Prophet raised the status of *'ilm* and *'ulama* (scholars) in many famous *hadiths*, including the following: "The virtue of knowledge is higher than the virtue of worship," and "The status of the scholar compared to the worshiper is like [the splendor of] the full moon compared to the [tiny] planets [in the sky]; indeed, scholars are the heirs of the prophets, who did not leave any money behind but knowledge, and whoever acquires it has acquired great value." Various levels of religious knowledge are required of Muslims, individually (*fard 'ayn*, i.e. obligatory) for the correct practice of Islam, or collectively (*fard kifayah*,[4] i.e. sufficient group acquisition) for the appropriate handling of new issues or queries.

But what does *'ilm* encompass? Golshani says: "We believe that the spectrum of knowledge recommended by Islam is very wide. It includes both specifically religious teachings and those branches of knowledge that are beneficial to the welfare of individuals and human societies" (Golshani 2013). He insists that *'ilm* as described in the Qur'an is *not* (as some traditional scholars claim) limited to the religious fields that are obligatory for Muslims to know about. In fact, Golshani simply rejects the traditional classification of knowledge into religious and nonreligious; he notes that in the Qur'an (e.g., 39:9, 96:5, 16:70), *'ilm* is presented in its most general meaning. Golshani adopts the twentieth-century Iranian scholar Murtaza Mutahhari's principle: "Islam's comprehensiveness and finality as a religion demands that every field of knowledge that is beneficial for an Islamic society be regarded as a part and parcel of the 'religious sciences'" (Mutahhari 1922: 137).

Ziauddin Sardar, another important author whose ideas on Islam and science will be expanded on in the next section, fully supports this holistic philosophy of knowledge in Islam. He writes:

> Polymaths, like Al-Biruni, Al-Jahiz [and ten others he mentions by name], and thousands of other scholars are not an exception but the general rule in Muslim civilization. The Islamic civilization of the classical period was remarkable for the number of polymaths it produced. This is seen as a testimony to the homogeneity of Islamic philosophy of science and its emphasis on synthesis, interdisciplinary investigations and multiplicity of methods. (Sardar 2006a: 112)

Muslim scholars often say that the first acquisition of *'ilm* by humans occurred when just after creating him, God taught Adam "all the names" (interpreted as "concepts") and asked him to recite them, which he did successfully, thereby proving to the angels that humans had a distinct capacity that made them superior to all other creatures and worthy of carrying God's mission on Earth. Man can thus learn anything – in principle. Conversely, this means that nature can be understood.

Furthermore, knowledge is vast and encompasses many fields. In the many Qur'anic verses which relate to knowledge and its acquisition, one finds a variety of terms pointing to a hierarchy of methods: listening (in the sense of understanding), observing, contemplating, reasoning, considering, reflecting,

---

[4] *Fard 'ayn* and *fard kifaya* are Islamic juristic (*fiqh*) categories: The first refers to obligations on each individual (e.g., prayer and fasting); the second refers to actions that are incumbent upon the community (e.g., medicine), and if a sufficient number have carried them out, the rest of the community are exempted from engaging in them.

and so on, each occurring a dozen times or more. Examples include: "And He has subjected to you, as from Him, all that is in the heavens and on earth: Behold, in that are Signs indeed for those who reflect" (45:13). The exploration and study of nature is highly encouraged and recommended: "Say: Consider what is in the heavens and the earth" (10:101) and "Say: Travel in the land and see how He originated creation" (29:20). Golshani remarks:

> In fact the main reason that our great scholars, in the glorious period of Islamic civilization, paid attention to foreign (especially Greek) sciences was due to the Qur'an's emphasis on the study of nature ... Al-Biruni [973–1048] has explicitly stated that the motive behind his research in the scientific fields is Allah's Words in the Qur'an: "Those who reflect on the creation of the heavens and the earth (and say): Our Lord! Thou hast not created this in vain! Glory be to Thee" (3:191). (Golshani 2003a: 154)

Similarly, the illustrious astronomer Al-Battani (858–929) wrote: "By focusing attention, observation, and extensive thought on astronomical phenomena, one is able to prove the unicity of God and to recognize the extent of the Creator's might as well as His wide wisdom and delicate design" (Mujahed 2004: 100). Golshani refers to Al-Biruni's insistence on the necessity of justifying every claim "by clear proof," citing the Qur'anic verse (8:2): "That he who lives might live by clear proof, and most surely Allah is Hearing, Knowing" (Golshani 2003b: 142). Likewise, Ibn Sina (980–1037) stressed the importance of requiring proof: "He who gets used to believing without proof has slipped out of his natural humanness" (Golshani 2003b: 126).

2 Islam and Science: The Debates So Far

Brief Historical Review: When Did the Debates Start?

Even a brief historical review of the debates around science/knowledge/philosophy and Islam requires us to go back to the genesis of the Islamic scientific tradition and how it was considered in relation to Islam's principles. There is an ongoing debate among historians on whether that tradition was jump-started by the "translation movement," that is, the great effort to bring the knowledge of ancient cultures and civilizations (mainly Indian and Greek) to Arabic, to be digested and improved upon by Islamic scholars. We must remark that labeling scholars as "Islamic" does not refer to their religious identity, but simply their belonging to the Islamic civilization. Many were not Muslim, and most were not Arabs, but the overwhelming majority of their works were written in Arabic, hence the tradition is sometimes referred to as "Arabic." Some historians, however, insist that some scientific activity (astronomy mainly, more precisely "prophetic cosmology," see Iqbal 2007: 29–32) was taking place before the translation movement exploded.

Contemporary historian Ahmad Dallal insists that we should start any exploration of the relation between Islam and science by reviewing the various exegeses of the Qur'an, the incorporation of scientific knowledge in those works, and the status such knowledge was given (Dallal 2012). A famous and influential work that represents perhaps the strongest engagement of classical exegesis (*tafsir*) with science (of the time) is that of Fakhr Al-Din Al-Razi (1150–1210). He was fully familiar with the scientific (particularly astronomical) knowledge and philosophical debates of his period and did not hesitate to include that knowledge in his commentaries on various verses, particularly those relating to "the marvel(s) of creation," a leitmotiv in Qur'anic exegeses.

Classical Qur'anic commentaries often highlighted the numerous, varied, and beautiful phenomena of nature that are mentioned and taken to point to the Creator. Moreover, classical exegetists insisted on God's power in making the world as He wished. Philosophers and theologians, on the other hand, discussed what reason and purpose there must have been for God to have made the world in this form, for the Qur'an itself says: "We have not created the heavens and the earth and all that is between them in vain, that is the view of the disbelievers" (38:27). The questions of contingency and teleology (purpose and "final" goals) in the creation of the world and its present phenomena were to be a prime topic of debate as well as a motivation to explore and try to understand the world.

Most importantly, however, Dallal insists:

> Nowhere does one encounter the notion that a certain scientific fact or theory is predicted or even favored by the Qur'an. ... In these commentaries scientific knowledge is freely invoked and occasionally challenged. Yet the purpose of rejecting some scientific views is not to promote alternative ones, nor to assert the authority of the Qur'an at the expense of the various fields of science. In the absence of a clear statement in the Qur'an, one seeks answers to scientific questions in their respective fields. The contrary, however, is not true because the text is not science. When there is an apparent conflict between a Qur'anic text and a scientific fact, commentators do not present the Qur'anic text as the arbiter but simply try to explore the possibility of alternative scientific explanations and thus suggest that scientific knowledge on such points of contention is not categorical. (Dallal 2012: 33)

He concludes: "Thus it follows that religious knowledge and scientific knowledge are each assigned to their own compartments" (Dallal 2012: 33).

Muslim philosophers and "scientists" held interesting views on the relation of philosophy/science and Islam. Al-Biruni, devout as he was, explicitly stated that the Qur'anic injunctions to contemplate and explore God's creation were a prime motivation for his research (Golshani 2003a: 154). Additionally, he upheld a highly rigorous methodology, insisting on the obligation for scholars to justify every claim "by clear proof." Furthermore, he warned against letting one's religious beliefs influence one's scientific conclusions. Dallal notes: "Evidence from the writings of religious scholars suggests that Biruni's view was in conformity with prevalent views within Islamic discursive culture. This . . . further suggests a conceptual separation of science and religion in the mainstream classical Islamic culture" (Dallal 2012: 29).

Al-Ghazali (1058–1111), the famous and influential Islamic scholar, is largely (and simplistically) portrayed as an enemy of philosophy and of science as he warned against some of their claims, and even condemned the philosophers who made claims that, in his view, blatantly contradicted Islamic dogmas. In reality, Al-Ghazali condemned metaphysical ideas such as God's ignorance of "particulars" (details of phenomena), the nonbodily resurrection of humans (on the Day of Judgment), and the past eternity of the world, ideas that he deemed in total conflict with Islamic beliefs and in no way justifiable by philosophical or scientific inferences. Additionally, he stressed that the sciences (mathematics and astronomy in particular) often provide strong knowledge that can be confirmed, thus (conservative) scholars must not reject them wholesale just because (some) philosophers have drawn nonjustifiable conclusions from them.

Finally, Al-Ghazali is widely "known" to have rejected the principle of causation, or, more precisely, "secondary causes," that is, the idea that phenomena are caused by conditions or occurrences in nature, which then inexorably lead to effects or results that are (deterministically) predictable.[5] Al-Ghazali claims that there is enough consistency in natural phenomena, due to God's "habits" (*al-sunan al-ilahiyya*) – and indeed, the Qur'an speaks of God's habits being "unchanging" (Q 33:62) – to enable people to understand nature's workings; however, it is God who acts in the world at every instant and on each phenomenon, minor or major, not some causal nexus.

Ibn Rushd (1126–1198), who responded at length and in detail to Al-Ghazali (see Averroes 2008 and 2017), accepted God's right and power to act wherever He wishes (i.e. the possibility of miracles), but insisted that nature is ordered in such a way as to preserve causal relations. For him, abandoning the principle of causality is tantamount to abandoning reason. In his *Decisive Treatise* on the connection or harmony between philosophy and Islamic law, Ibn Rushd strongly reiterated a principle that other major scholars (including Al-Ghazali) had stated (but not applied clearly and systematically): If sufficiently

---

[5] This is, in fact, a disputed point. Malay theologian Muhammad Afifi Al Akiti has reassessed Al-Ghazali's widely accepted "opposition" to causality (or at least to secondary causes) based on Al-Ghazali's important but less-well-known work *Al-Madnun bihi 'ala ghayri ahlihi* ("That which is restricted from those unfit for it") (Al-Akiti 2016).

proven knowledge from philosophy or science conflicts with the statements of the Qur'an, it is necessary to resort to hermeneutics (*ta'wil*), that is, to reinterpret the Text, harmonizing it with established knowledge (philosophical or scientific).

For all Muslim thinkers (Ibn Sina, Al-Ghazali, Ibn Rushd, and others), there is unity and harmony between the rational process of knowing the world and proper reading of the Revelation. However, Muslim thinkers differ on the appropriate approach to ensure such unity and harmony.

Modern Science and Its Impact

Science has changed substantially and in several ways since medieval times. It has made leaps in theory (thanks to advanced mathematical tools such as calculus, numerical analysis, probabilistic and statistical analysis, and more) and in experiment (the range and sophistication of instruments is too immense to describe here). Science has also invited philosophers to help define and refine its methods, where and however appropriate. Furthermore, philosophy of science has helped clarify something that was promoted by some scientists in medieval times (e.g. Al-Biruni and Ibn Al-Haytham), namely that science must remain *naturalistic*, that is, only invoking natural causes and factors (no supernatural agents) when attempting to explain a natural phenomenon. This will be one of the main contentious issues in the science and religion debates, particularly in the Islamic context. Last but not least, thanks to the increased speed in communication, peer reviewing of scientists' works has become more efficient, helping filter out mistaken ideas and results.

The Muslim world's experience with modern science is directly related to its encounters with modernity in the last two or three centuries. By the middle of the eighteenth century, the Muslim/Ottoman world became aware of the important advances that Europe was making in various scientific fields (astronomy, i.e. the Copernican revolution, physics with Newton and others, medicine, and other fields).[6] This new knowledge and its applications (new technology, including military) were worrisome developments; indeed, colonialism was soon to follow.

The dazzling Western advance in science and technology both before and after colonialism raised a perplexing question: Why did that scientific leap not take place in the Islamic world, before colonialism (eighteenth–nineteenth centuries) or after independence? Is there something in the culture/religion of the Muslim world that has made the methods of science difficult to

---

[6] See, in particular, the works of the polymath Ibrahim Hakki Erzurumi (1703–1780), among others.

adopt? In a famous lecture given at the Sorbonne in 1883, Ernest Renan (1823–1892), a French orientalist, historian, and philologist, answered the question bluntly:

> Islam is the disdain of science, the suppression of civil society; it is the appalling simplicity of the Semitic mind, shrinking the human brain, closing it to any delicate idea, to any fine feeling, to any rational research, to present it only with an eternal tautology: God is God. The future, Gentlemen, is therefore in Europe and in Europe alone. (Renan 1862: 27–28)

He added that the scientific development that had occurred during the Islamic civilization was merely tolerated by Islam, and it dried up after a few centuries.

The same question, along with similar yet gentler answers, resurfaced at the end of the twentieth century, when, after some fifty years of independence, the Islamic world was producing less than 5 percent of the scientific and technological developments of humanity. Is there something in Islam or in modern science that makes the two difficult to marry? Muslim reformers of the nineteenth–twentieth centuries (Sayyid Ahmad Khan, Jamal Al-Din Al-Afghani, Muhammad Abduh, M. Rashid Rida, Muhammad Iqbal, Said Nursi, Süleyman Ateş, and others) tried to ignite Muslim development in science and technology, while believing that the problem was deeper, rooted in Muslims' adoption of a less dynamic and more conformist and fatalistic religious worldview. Their answer consisted in a call and drive to "reopen the gates of *ijtihad*" (individual or collective effort to address new issues). However, they also noted that science was being presented in a materialistic garb, to which Al-Afghani reacted, for example, with his book *The Refutation of the Materialists*, first published in Persian in 1881, then in Arabic in 1886. The "reform" took on different forms according to each "reformer": a return to the "sources" (according to Ibn Abdelwahab, Hasan El-Banna, and other Salafists or traditionalists), to a modernity that can be compatible with Islam (according to Khan), that is, rational, scientific, universalist, or other "programs." Internal debates, if not fights, broke out: Al-Afghani labeled Khan a *nechari* ("naturalist"), that is, close to materialism. Ibn Abdelwahab and his followers accused everyone else of *bid'a* (innovation), that is, introducing into Islam what was never part of it, and so on. A "middle path" was taken by Said Nursi (1877–1960), a Turkish reformer who accepted and appreciated the ability of modern science to discover unimaginable wonders of the universe, which for him made it a good conduit to knowing God and worshiping Him. Nursi wanted Muslims to pursue a double program: leading a deeply spiritual life, partly fueled by contemplating natural and cosmic phenomena, and strictly following the Qur'anic injunctions, which make up the moral code for life.

At about the same time, a new approach to Qur'anic *tafsir* was beginning to appear. Some scholars, most famously Muhammad Abduh (1849–1905), began using new scientific information (about bacteria, planetary orbits, etc.) to interpret some verses more "scientifically and rationally"; this approach came to be known as *tafsir 'ilmi* ("scientific exegesis"). Others, starting with the physician Muhammad Al-Iskandarani (d. 1889) and the religious scholar Tantawi Jawhari (1870–1940), both Egyptian, began claiming the existence of scientific content in the Qur'an, predating modern knowledge and discoveries; this came to be known as *i'jaz 'ilmi* ("miraculous scientific content" in the Qur'an, and later in the Sunnah as well). Indeed, Al-Iskandarani can be considered the founder of *i'jaz 'ilmi*, which by the late twentieth century became an extraordinarily popular cultural movement in the Arab-Muslim world. In 1880, Al-Iskandarani published *The Unveiling of the Luminous Secrets of the Qur'an in Which Are Discussed Celestial Bodies, the Earth, Animals, Plants, and Minerals* (*Kashf al-asrar al-nuraniyya al Qur'aniyya fi ma yata 'allaqu bi-l-ajram al-samawiyya wa-l-ardiyya wa-l-hayawanat wa-l-nabatat wa-l-jawahir al-ma 'daniyya*). He followed this up in 1883 with *Divine Secrets in the World of Vegetation and Minerals and in the Characteristics of Animals* (*Tibyan al-asrar al rabbaniyya fi al-nabatat wa-l-ma 'adin wa-l-khawass al-hayawaniyya*). In 1931, Tantawi Jawhari took things to another level by publishing a twenty-six-volume encyclopedic exegesis of the Qur'an titled *Pearls from the Tafsir of the Noble Qur'an* (*Al-Jawahir fi tafsir Al-Qur'an Al-Karim*), complete with an assortment of illustrations and tables.

In these books, and countless others that were to follow in the next 100 years or so, Qur'anic verses (revealed over 1,400 years ago) are claimed to refer to scientific discoveries – and later also technological inventions – that had only been made in the last century or two. Indeed, the *i'jaz*[7] literature came to claim that atoms, genetics, pulsars, black holes, the speed of light, the ages of Earth and of the universe, the phone and fax, email, radio, and TV were all in the Qur'an, if one just read the verses with a discerning eye. As we will see in another section, a boost to this phenomenon came in the 1970s with the work of the French physician Maurice Bucaille (1920–1998). One can safely state that the Muslim world now displays (for reasons that warrant careful scrutiny) a veritable infatuation with his "theory," currently being taught in many curricula, from middle school to doctorate levels.

Last but not least in our brief historical review of the genesis of the debates in Islam and the sciences is the reception of Darwin's theory of evolution. While Muslim scholars and intellectuals became aware of Darwin's theory soon after it

---

[7] We will, for short, use *i'jaz* to refer to *i'jaz 'ilmi*, although we should note that *i'jaz tout court* refers to the classical Islamic claim that the Qur'an is miraculous, at least in its linguistic aspects.

was published (in 1859), for all intents and purposes, its wider impact and disputes would only become evident well into the twentieth century. Some early books, particularly those of Al-Afghani (*The Refutation of the Materialists*, in 1881, previously mentioned) and of the Lebanese theologian Husayn Al-Jisr (1845–1909), discussed evolution in the context of "materialist" theories. The burgeoning Arab science magazines[8] of the day also contributed to the discussion. Although it was known for its substantial discussion of and thoughtful reaction to Darwin's theory, Al-Jisr's 1887 book *A Hamidian*[9] *Essay on the Veracity of the Islamic Religion and the Veracity of the Islamic Canon Law* (*Al-Risala al-Hamidiyya fi haqiqat al-diyana al-Islamiyya wa-haqiqat al-Shari'a al-Muhammadiyya*) was in fact a defense of Islamic theology and jurisprudence against "materialist" theories, of which evolution could be viewed as one example, since it provided a naturalistic explanation for the appearance of living creatures without reference to God. Al-Jisr's position, however, was quite interesting: (a) Darwin's theory remains unproven; (b) if it does become established with strong evidence, Islam will not have a problem with it as long as it does not deny the central principle of a creator; indeed, verses can be reinterpreted, using the same principle that Ibn Rushd and others had invoked to harmonize Islam with rational knowledge; (c) it is highly doubtful that humans could be part of such an evolutionary scheme; (d) more generally, explaining phenomena naturally is acceptable, if these explanations are seen as "God's ways."

As the historian Adel Ziadat explains in his excellent review of the early reception of 'evolution' in the Arab world, the debates focused more on philosophical, religious, and social implications than on the scientific aspects of the theory (Ziadat 1986). Still, we should stress that the positions covered a wide spectrum, ranging from simplistic rejection to acceptance *in toto*. (Some Arab secularists saw in Darwinism the embodiment of the modern, scientific spirit of the times.) However, in the second half of the twentieth century, Darwin's theory came to be almost uniformly rejected by Muslims: laypersons and educated people, religious scholars and other intellectuals alike. In a sign that science had acquired a very high status and philosophical or religious critiques of evolution would no longer suffice, Muslims began looking for Western, scientific-sounding creationist material. The antievolution banner was picked up by the highly controversial Turkish figure Harun Yahya (pen name of Adnan Oktar, b. 1956) and his group, who produced voluminous materials (books, videos, websites) in multiple languages,

---

[8] For example, *Al-Muqtataf* (1876–1952), *Al-Hilal* (1892–1930), and *Al-Mashriq* (1898–1930).

[9] "Hamidian" referred to the Ottoman sultan Abdulhamid, to whom the book was dedicated.

distributed worldwide free of charge. The materials were often crude adoptions of Western creationist sources, full of scientifically incorrect arguments.[10] Only a few lone Muslim voices tried to redress the debate by both providing accurate scientific information and presenting more varied and subtle theological and philosophical opinions.

A Map of the Schools of Thought in Islam and Science

Sayyid Ahmad Khan

Perhaps the first serious encounter and response by Muslim intellectuals to modern science was that of Sir Sayyid Ahmad Khan (1817–1898), the Indian thinker, educationist, and reformer, who formulated a modernist theology. Confronted with European colonial modernity, he was convinced that attaining a level of education and mastery of science and technology comparable to that of the colonists was crucial for Islamic revival in general and the welfare of his fellow Indian Muslims and their political empowerment more particularly. In 1875, he established the Muhammadan Anglo-Oriental College (Aligarh, India), modeled after Cambridge University, later named Aligarh Muslim University (1920), which has remained a major center of education to this day. Khan had to defuse the criticism and disparagement of Islam as a superstitious and hence inferior creed. He stressed that Christianity and Islam conveyed a similar moral message, and he presented Islam as conforming with human nature, intrinsically rational and compatible with science. For Khan, who stressed the need for *ijtihad* (renewed intellectual effort) and contrasted it with *taqlid* (upholding tradition), catching up with rationality and modernity meant returning to the spirit of the original and true Islam – which was intellectually dynamic and creative – and achieving greatness, the possibility of which was demonstrated by the political and scientific glories of Islamic history.

A major conceptual challenge was represented by the narratives of miracles. Since Khan described the laws of nature as "divine covenants," he regarded their supposed violations as implying God's untrustworthiness. Rejecting any conflict between the Word of God (Scripture) and the Work of God (nature), Khan suggested that non-Quranic, folk-miracle stories must simply be moral tales, while Qur'anic accounts could be read as descriptions of events that actually took place, yet without violating the laws of nature. For instance, *al-isra' wa-l-mi'raj* (the Prophet's journey to Jerusalem and to the heavens in one night) could be interpreted as a dream (Parray 2015).

---

[10] For a thorough discussion of Yahya's activities and ideas, see Ross Solberg 2013.

Muhammad Abduh

Abduh (1849–1905), the renowned and influential Egyptian Muslim scholar, may be considered the leader of the Islamic reform movement that engulfed the Arab world between the mid-nineteenth and the mid-twentieth centuries. Abduh realized that to revive the Islamic civilization and catch up and compete with the West, a double reform needed to be ignited: revising the Islamic legal system and basing it on pragmatic principles (including social customs) and reviewing one's understanding of the Qur'an on the basis of rational inquiries and interpretations of both the historical information and the natural phenomena mentioned therein. Abduh insisted that Islam (particularly the Qur'an) distinguishes itself by its insistence on rational argumentation/demonstration. Thus, it is not just that reason and science are compatible and in harmony with Islam; the latter is based on reason in all its dimensions (theology, jurisprudence, etc.).

Abduh became famous for the reforms he pushed for as a high judge, a member of the board of Al-Azhar, and Mufti of Egypt: girls' education, modernized curricula in public and religious schools, progressive *fatwas* (e.g. that polygamy is permissible but should be exceedingly rare today), and reinterpretation of various passages of the Qur'an. He published commentaries on at least one third of the Qur'an, but died before finishing his work, a task that his disciple Muhammad Rashid Rida undertook afterwards. One famous example of Abduh's approach to the Qur'an in the realm of natural or scientific subjects is his interpretation of the "birds" that "pelted" the Aksumite army over Mecca (Q 105:1–5) in 570 CE: He suggests that the "birds" were mosquitoes or flies that carried microbes. In another passage, Abduh comments on Noah's flood: "No one who firmly believes in religion should reject something demonstrated by the literal meaning of the verses, and *hadith*s whose *isnad*s [transmissions] are trustworthy, in favor of this interpretation, except by rational evidence which positively shows that the literal meaning is not the one intended by the text" (Abduh 1972: 512–513).[11]

Al-Faruqi and the "Islamization of Knowledge"

One original proposal on how Islam and science should be related was advanced in the late 1970s by the Palestinian-American thinker Ismail Raji Al-Faruqi (1921–1986): a full-fledged "Islamization of knowledge." Al-Faruqi asked himself why the Muslim community, or *Ummah*, was in such a state of weakness and fragmentation despite its enormous potential. His answer: because it had been

---

[11] Translation by Aziz Al-Azmeh, who acknowledges a draft translation by Dr. Ronald Buckley (Al-Azmeh 1996: 118).

contaminated by Western, destructive principles such as nationalism, which he saw as a "despicable Western virus" (Al-Faruqi 1995: xiv), and skepticism (the opposite of faith and trust), which he blamed on science, for its success was "seen as the continuing victory of the empirical over the religious mind" (Al-Faruqi 1995: 39). For Al-Faruqi, the *Ummah* could be rejuvenated and unified by returning to genuine Islamic principles, which were epistemological as well as ethical. Scientists should be guided by faith in God, *tawhid*, as the antidote to skepticism.[12] Moreover, Al-Faruqi stressed the Qur'anic conceptualization of the human being as *khalifa*, or God's representative and "tenant" or "gerent" on Earth, as conducive to a more environmentally responsible behavior (Al-Faruqi 1995: 57–59). All disciplines, according to Al-Faruqi, had to be "Islamized," that is, reformed (in fact, *recast*) according to Islamic principles (the above and others), then developed and disseminated by a network of Muslim scholars in academic and political institutions.

The idea of "Islamizing" knowledge and science was undermined by serious conceptual and methodological problems. To begin with, the whole discourse seemed to rely on the presupposition that it would be possible to somehow extract from the Qur'an clear epistemological principles that would help reform knowledge, even though the Islamizers themselves insisted that the Qur'an was being read through an exegetical tradition that had been rotting for centuries. Moreover, would the Islamization of knowledge and science entail the rejection of principles and achievements produced by non-Muslim philosophers and scientists? And would previously obtained scientific results have to be changed with the adoption of new "Islamized" methods? Finally, it appears that while Al-Faruqi thought he was addressing core methodological issues of science, he was in reality prescribing an Islamization of the scientists' *worldview*. In other words, he was asking scientists to interpret their activity, object of study, and results through Islamic concepts. This, however, is far from being a genuine "Islamization" of science. Still, the idea of Islamizing science has survived to date and is being taken up in Malaysia, in particular (Ssekamanya et al. 2011), and in Indonesia, to some extent (Kurniawan n.d.). The International Institute of Islamic Thought that Al-Faruqi established in the USA in 1981 still exists, although its mission seems to have been watered down from its original ideals and goals.

Seyyed Hossein Nasr: Scientia Sacra

A notable and radical critique of science was elaborated by the Iranian-American philosopher Seyyed Hossein Nasr (b. 1933). He earned a degree in physics at MIT as the first Iranian undergraduate to be admitted to the

---

[12] "God is the *necessary condition* of all natural science" (Al-Faruqi 1995: 53; emphasis added).

institution, then obtained a master's degree in geology and geophysics at Harvard University, followed by a PhD in the history of science. He was, however, influenced by antimodernist philosophical views (Sedgwick 2004) such as those of the Italian-American philosopher Giorgio de Santillana (1902–1974), and came to doubt that physics truly allowed one to understand reality.

One element in Nasr's life and thought that is of great importance in understanding his conception of knowledge and science is Sufi mysticism, that is the teaching according to which certain spiritual practices and rituals can lead to direct contact with God. Nasr is indeed a Sufi master. Additionally, he was strongly influenced by "perennialist" authors, such as Ananda Kentish Coomaraswamy (1877–1947), René Guénon (1886–1951), Henry Corbin (1903–1978), Frithjof Schuon (1907–1998), and Titus Burckhardt (1908–1984). In their view, different religions essentially converge on, and perennially have been conveying, the same message: Humans derive from a transcendent God. Following such realizations, humans can (indeed should) restore contact with the divine. Islam, according to Nasr, stands out from other religions by virtue of being the last revelation received by humanity (Nasr 1993: 103) and by its emphasis of the unicity of God (Nasr 1993: 12). Additionally, Nasr holds that humans are endowed with a faculty, or a "supernaturally natural function" that he calls the intellect, through which they can "know the Absolute," that is, reconnect with God and access levels of consciousness superior to daily, ordinary perceptions (Nasr 1981: 2–5). Nasr regards Western thought, including the natural sciences, as characterized by the negation and rejection of God, as well as by fragmentariness. Such major flaws, he thinks, have led to the debasement of the human being and the physical destruction of the natural world, while creating an illusion of progress (see, for instance, Nasr & Iqbal 2007). The reconnection with God can heal such ills, and should inspire and nourish the introduction of an alternative way of attaining and constructing knowledge, which Nasr calls *scientia sacra*, whereby nature and "reality" are inseparable from the sacred.

This can already be glimpsed in Nasr's first, seminal work, *An Introduction to Islamic Cosmological Doctrines* (Nasr 1964). In it, he covers a spectrum of classical (medieval) Islamic cosmologies: the neo-Pythagorean and hermetic worldview of the *Ikhwan as-Safa*;[13] Al-Biruni's mathematical and astronomical approach; and Ibn Sina's Aristotelian cosmo-philosophy. It is perhaps sufficiently indicative to note that in this work, the words "Sufis" and "Sufism" (Islamic mystics and mysticism) appear forty-five and twenty times

---

[13] Literally: the Brethren of Purity, a society of Muslim philosophers active in Basra (Iraq) in the ninth or tenth century CE.

and "Gnosis" (illumination or spiritual insight) and "Gnostic" appear thirty and forty-four times, respectively. Nasr sees spirituality as infusing all Islamic conceptions and works, first in cosmology (a much broader field than modern science), then later in the rest of Islamic science.

Nasr's writings stand out for their depth and richness. He commands respect for his academic achievements, his prolificness, and his advocacy of interfaith dialogue. However, Nasr's discussion of science is problematic. For instance, it includes the rejection of Darwinian evolution, whose acceptance, according to him, requires more faith than religion does (see Nasr 1982, 1993: 156; Nasr & Iqbal 2007). The concept of *scientia sacra* is also ambiguous and suspicious in several ways. In particular, it seemingly entails the reinstatement of fields such as alchemy and astrology. This makes *scientia sacra* untenable. Finally, while the Sufi experience may provide its practitioners windows onto supernatural levels of reality, it is difficult to see how such an experience, and such levels, could be integrated within the scientific enterprise, which insists on objectivity and universality.

Naquib Al-Attas

There are strong similarities between the Malaysian Islamic philosopher Syed Muhammad Naquib Al-Attas (b. 1931) and Seyyed H. Nasr. Both combined deep study and knowledge of Islamic tradition (Sufism and metaphysics, in particular) with that of Western thought, and both promoted a philosophy of knowledge/ science that insisted on integrating rational methods with larger intellectual and spiritual ways of knowing. Both Al-Attas and Nasr have claimed paternity of the idea/program of "Islamic science," which essentially consists of considering "reality" as a multiple physical, spiritual, and psychological space. This reality can be explored in various ways, without negating revelation and without insisting on purely rational and empirical methods, as modern science does. In Al-Attas "Islamic philosophy of science" (science being understood as *'ilm*, i.e., much more broadly and combining various fields, including mysticism), God is the ultimate source of knowledge, hence channels and communications with the divine are perfectly valid methods of discovery and cognition (Al-Attas 1989). Personal and subjective means of knowing can then be confirmed by Revelation and/or coherent relation to other truths, whether arrived at internally or externally. Al-Attas also recommends the adoption in science of the double Qur'anic exegetical approach of *tafsir* (explaining the apparent meaning of verses) and *ta'wil* (interpreting verses and finding hidden meanings). Modern science, in this conception, limits itself to a *tafsir* of natural and cosmic phenomena, whereas Islamic science/ *'ilm* goes beyond it and integrates spiritual practices and symbols (see Setia 2003 and references therein) to interpret the world.

Sardar and the Ijmalis: *Islamic (Ethical) Science*

Another important contribution to the debates in Islam and science was offered by a heterogeneous group of intellectuals[14] who called themselves the *Ijmalis*,[15] loosely led by the British-Pakistani thinker Ziauddin Sardar (b. 1951). Sardar too earned a degree in the sciences (physics and information science at City University in London). He is known as a widely knowledgeable scholar, an analytical thinker, a prolific author, and a provocative (and witty) public intellectual. Sardar and the *Ijmalis* did not believe that science is value-free, but rather that the perceptions on which science is founded are subjective; they did not, however, advocate extreme relativism, maintaining that consensus keeps relativism in check (Sardar 1989: 156–161). Most importantly, in their view, science should be oriented toward solving practical problems and be relevant to Muslim (and other) societies. Not unlike Al-Faruqi and Nasr, the *Ijmalis* regarded Western science as destructive and in a state of crisis (Sardar 1984: 1–12); Sardar likened contemporary science to the "touch of Midas" whose "ability to do a great good for mankind seems to be overshadowed by its even greater capacity to do evil" (Sardar 1984: 1).

Sardar has continuously and consistently criticized the whole *i'jaz* trend, especially since it ended up being pushed to extremes with far-fetched claims of the Qur'an containing references to relativity and quantum mechanics. Most importantly, *i'jaz* gives to science the power of validating the Qur'an's divine origin, while Muslims should consider it "a priori valid and eternal"; moreover, scientific theories are often revised, and scientists sometimes are just wrong. This does not mean, Sardar insists, that the Qur'an and science have no relation whatsoever, but that this relation should be conceptualized more carefully. The Qur'an should be regarded as a God-given book containing ethical precepts and an invitation to appreciate, develop, and practice science and technology, but not as an encyclopedia of scientific facts (Sardar 1985).

Despite having some points in common with their critiques and objectives,[16] Sardar expressed strong opposition to Al-Faruqi's and Nasr's plans. He outspokenly, if respectfully, criticized Al-Faruqi's ideas early on, right after the publication of his ideas on the Islamization of knowledge. Sardar, then barely in his mid-twenties, going against the grain of the intellectuals who had received

---

[14] Leif Stenberg lists among the *Ijmalis* the anthropologist Merryl Wyn Davies (1948–2021), the geologist S. Parvez Manzoor, and the biologist Munawar Ahmed Anees (Stenberg 1996: 48–50). For Sardar's own reconstruction of the *Ijmali* movement, see Sardar 2004: 207–208.

[15] "*Ijmalis*" is a term they coined using the Arabic words for holistic and beautiful.

[16] The similarities between the three authors' respective approaches are extensively explored in Stenberg's monograph *The Islamization of Science* (Stenberg 1996). Significantly, ideas from Nasr and Sardar were combined by some Indian authors in the 1980s, a group of thinkers known as the Aligarh School (Kirmani 2015; Bigliardi 2016).

Al-Faruqi's ideas with enthusiasm, explained that the whole enterprise seemed to him methodologically flawed. He described it as a futile "face-lift" operated on disciplines that were imbibed with materialistic metaphysics; ultimately, such an attempt would leave the dichotomy between "secular" and "Islamic" science untouched.[17] As for Nasr, Sardar thought that his mystic approach was elitist, his metaphysics was confused, and his historical references were plagued by omissions and errors (Sardar 1989: 114–134). In the end, Al-Faruqi, Nasr, and Sardar's ideas and programs did not have any wide impact beyond academic and intellectual circles. It seems more likely that their contributions to, for instance, Islamic environmental ethics, were more of a reaction to, and re-elaboration on, popular as well as academic motifs of their times, shared with intellectuals coming from different backgrounds and whose influence has continued into the early twenty-first century.

Abdus Salam, Islam, and "Universal Science"

A relevant, although rather elusive, figure in the debates on Islam and science is the great Pakistani scientist Muhammad Abdus Salam (1926–1996), who was awarded the Nobel Prize in Physics in 1979 with Steven Weinberg (1933–2021) and Sheldon Glashow (b. 1932).[18] In addition to his accomplishments as a scientist, Abdus Salam must be remembered for the initiatives he conducted to support scientific education and international research, particularly for developing countries, such as the founding of the International Centre for Theoretical Physics in Trieste (Italy) in 1964, which he directed until 1993 and which now bears his name.[19] Abdus Salam has symbolic value as the first of only a few Muslim Nobel laureates in a scientific field, but he also contributed, with his pronouncements and writings, to the debates on Islam and science.

In his official Nobel Prize profile, one reads that Abdus Salam is "a devout Muslim,[20] whose religion does not occupy a separate compartment of his life; it is inseparable from his work and family life."[21] Scholarly assessments of his

---

[17] For a vivid report of the disagreement between the two intellectuals, see Sardar 2004: 196–203.

[18] For their important contributions on the unification of the weak and electromagnetic forces, see "Abdus Salam: Biographical. The Nobel Prize in Physics 1973," *The Nobel Prize*, n.d., www .nobelprize.org/prizes/physics/1979/salam/biographical/.

[19] See The Abdus Salam International Centre for Theoretical Physics homepage at www.ictp.it/ about-ictp.aspx.

[20] Abdus Salam always presented himself as "Muslim." His family belonged to the Ahmadiyya community, which the Pakistani government declared non-Muslim in 1974. Some individuals later defaced his tombstone by erasing the word "Muslim" from it. This is also alluded to in the title of Anand Kamalakar's 2018 documentary, *Salam: The First ****** Nobel Laureate* (Kailoola Productions).

[21] See "Abdus Salam: Biographical," n.d., at www.nobelprize.org/prizes/physics/1979/salam/bio graphical/.

intellectual profile vary widely, however; Martin Riexinger has examined Abdus Salam's life, ideas, and accomplishments and concluded that he "kept his personal religious beliefs and his professional scientific work clearly apart," adding "it is impossible to detect any hint to suggest that the former influenced the latter" (Riexinger 2009: 319). Ismaël Omarjee has devoted an entire monograph to the discussion of the interplay of religious and scientific thought in Abdus Salam's work, suggesting that this interplay was crucial (Omarjee 2021). Abdus Salam did claim that the Qur'an had inspired his research, and referred to the Islamic concept of unity as an attractive idea for a Muslim physicist.[22] He also wrote that, while working toward the unification paradigm, he may have been "unconsciously motivated by [his] background as a Muslim" (Salam 1991: x). It should be added, however, that in another text Abdus Salam *downplayed* the role of faith in the research that earned him the Nobel Prize and remarked that an agnostic colleague had independently arrived at the same results (actually, both Weinberg and Glashow were atheists); on the one hand, he declared that he had a strong awareness of the link between his faith and his activity as a scientist, but he fully acknowledged, on the other hand, that such activity, in general, is not directly linked to (a) faith (Vauthier 1990: 71–72).

Abdus Salam also suggested that, although different societies may choose to emphasize specific disciplines, "the traditions and the modalities of science are universal" (Salam 1984: 194). In other words, while suggesting that Islam had inspired *his own* scientific endeavors, he stressed that science is universal in nature and certainly did not need to be Islamically reformed. Therefore, in Abdus Salam's perception, Islam, like other faiths, could enjoy a "harmonious complementarity" with science. He also rejected the idea that "modern science must lead to 'rationalism,' and eventually apostasy [*sic*]" (Salam 1984: 183). While admitting that certain kinds of metaphysics could collide with science, he also emphasized that science, as opposed to metaphysics, is characterized by reliance on empirical verification and self-consistency, and that its "conceptual edifice" is "provisional" (Salam 1984: 185–187).

In sum, Abdus Salam's discussion of science and religion is philosophically rather cursory. The fragmentary ideas that he advanced about Islam and science, in addition to serving his autobiographical narrative, provided a rhetorical wrapping rather than a solid theoretical base for his vigorous advocacy of the improvement of the quality of scientific research, the improvement of science education, and the furthering of scientific endeavor in the Muslim world (see, for instance, Salam 1986), a cause for which he advanced initiatives and projects that were successful to some extent.[23]

---

[22] Abdus Salam can be heard making this point himself in Kamalakar's documentary (mentioned in n. 20).

[23] For a comprehensive discussion of Salam's take on science and religion, see also Bigliardi 2022.

I'jaz 'ilmi: *Maurice Bucaille, Keith Moore, and Zaghloul El-Naggar*

In 1976, the French physician Maurice Bucaille (1920–1998) published the book *The Bible, the Qur'an and Science* (*La Bible, le Coran et la science*) which, perhaps going beyond the author's expectations and intentions, would become a milestone in the debates around Islam and modern science and turn him into a household name. Biographical information about Bucaille is scarce. In his books and interviews, one can read that he was educated at Catholic schools. After he became a successful gastroenterologist in Paris, his Muslim patients encouraged him to read the Qur'an in the original Arabic. Bucaille therefore began learning Arabic around 1970. He is generally thought to have converted to Islam; however, there is no strong evidence for this claim.[24]

His book is a comparative discussion of the Bible and the Qur'an with regard to science. On the one hand, Bucaille points out that the Bible does not withstand scientific and logical scrutiny: Several biblical passages clash with scientific information or contradict each other. For Bucaille, these imperfections simply confirm human interference in the transmission of the Bible's original text (which is what Muslims believe happened). On the other hand, he finds that the Qur'an is devoid of passages that conflict with logic or science; in fact, several of its descriptions of natural phenomena display a precision that, as they surpass human knowledge at the time of the Revelation, is suggestive of the book's divine origin.[25]

On other important issues surrounding science and religion, it is worth noting that Bucaille interpreted supernatural narratives (in the Bible as well as in the Qur'an) literally; that is, as events representing actual violations of natural laws (Bigliardi 2011). Additionally, in the book *What Is the Origin of Man?* (Bucaille 1981), he criticized and rejected Darwinian evolution, at least for humans. In his view, chance and time cannot explain the complexity of life; evolution is not supported by the fossil record, and it is based on an overstatement of the similarities between humans and apes. Bucaille advocated the idea that God periodically intervenes to modify living beings, a process which he called "creative evolution."

Another Westerner would soon become famous for similar reasons: the Canadian embryologist Keith Moore (1925–2019), who was convinced by the Yemeni Islamic preacher Abdul Majeed Azzindani (b. 1942) that some verses of the Qur'an were not only fully concordant with the knowledge contained in Moore's

---

[24] Bucaille's acquaintances in the Muslim world included the Egyptian president Muhammad Anwar El-Sadat (1918–1981) and his wife, as well as King Faisal of Saudi Arabia (1906–1975). It is, however, unknown exactly who or what initially sparked his interest in Arabic and the Qur'an. For a discussion of Bucaille's biography, see Bigliardi 2012.

[25] However, Bucaille denies that the *hadith*s are scientifically inerrant. See Bucaille 1976: 245–250.

embryology textbook, *The Developing Human*, but obviously predated it. Moore agreed to have his textbook published in a new Saudi special edition with a foreword in which he describes his astonishment upon noting the "accuracy" of the Qur'anic verses that describe the developmental stages of an embryo (Moore 1983).[26]

An important figure in the field of *i'jaz 'ilmi* who benefited from the new media that flourished after Bucaille's death is the Egyptian university professor and author Zaghloul El-Naggar (b. 1933), who obtained his PhD in geology from the University of Wales in 1963. After an academic career in the Gulf, he focused on *i'jaz* and was appointed chair of the Committee of Scientific Notions in the Qur'an, which is part of the Egyptian Ministry of Religious Affairs. He actually prefers the expression "scientific precision in the Qur'an," insisting that such "research" only be practiced by highly competent experts, and be based on solidly established scientific facts. He also emphasizes that nonmaterial entities and events mentioned in the Qur'an, such as angels and souls or the hereafter and resurrection, should be believed as a result of faith alone and not explained scientifically. El-Naggar has contributed numerous publications and TV shows on *i'jaz,* largely boosting its popularity in his native Egypt and across the Arab world, the region in which he is most impactful given that he mainly delivers his lectures in Arabic, although some of his work has been translated into other languages. He considers this work essential in rebutting atheism or the perception that religion is rendered obsolete by scientific and technological advancements.

El-Naggar upholds a literal interpretation of the supernatural miracles that punctuated the mission of messengers and prophets and emphasizes that such events do not occur for common mortals, not even "saints." He also merges his view of miraculous events with promoting *i'jaz 'ilmi,* such as his claim that the "splitting of the moon" was observed by American astronauts.[27] Interestingly, he prescribes that when different scientific hypotheses can be advanced to explain a given phenomenon, Muslim scientists should embrace the one that is most compatible with the Qur'an, a case in point being the big bang theory, which he sees as supported by the Qur'an. Finally, El-Naggar completely rejects biological evolution, claiming that fossils do not prove evolution, but simply that the Earth has been inhabited by successive forms of life.[28]

---

[26] For an analysis of how Azzindani capitalized on Moore's prestige to promote his interpretation of embryonic development, see Guénon 2019. For a wider and critical discussion of *i'jaz*, see Bigliardi 2014e and 2017a.

[27] This refers to the widely held but controversial claim that the Prophet and people around him witnessed a "splitting of the moon," "supported" by the Qur'an in 54:1–2, and El-Naggar's claims that US astronauts found evidence for it (El-Naggar 2010: 69–73). For a discussion of the various interpretations of the Qur'anic passage in question, see Görke 2010.

[28] For a thorough discussion of El-Naggar's activities and ideas, see Bigliardi 2014b: 103–132. El-Naggar illustrates his epistemological and interpretive principles in El-Naggar 2008: 7–27.

Pervez Hoodbhoy and "Secular Science"

The Pakistani physicist Pervez Hoodbhoy (b. 1950) considered Abdus Salam a role model and took his mentor's "universal science" to mean "secular science." His most important contribution to the debates is his 1991 monograph *Islam and Science: Religious Orthodoxy and the Battle for Rationality*; it was prefaced by Abdus Salam, who stated that he did not disagree with anything Hoodbhoy had written therein (Salam 1990: ix). Hoodbhoy strongly promotes the separation of science and religion. He stresses that "scientists are free to be as religious as they please, but science recognizes no laws outside its own" (Hoodbhoy 1991: 2) and defines religion as "reasoned and reasonable abdication of reason with regard to those questions which lie outside the reach of science, such as 'why does the universe exist?' or 'what is the purpose of life?'" (Hoodbhoy 1991: 137). According to him, provided that such a separation is implemented, science is equally "compatible" with a subjective, religious look and with atheism, as the interaction of Abdus Salam and Weinberg demonstrates, the two having been "geographically and ideologically remote from each other when they conceived the same theory of physics" (Hoodbhoy 1991: 78). He also states that Muslims' lack of material success should not be considered as decisive when evaluating the goodness or truth of their religion (Hoodbhoy 1991: 138–139).

Hoodbhoy sharply criticizes the major trends or schools of thought that we summarized above. The success of Bucaille's book and claims, he suggests, may largely be due to his appeal as a white man, still commanding respect for that reason, in spite of decolonization.[29] As to the *i'jaz* approach, Hoodbhoy agrees with Sardar's criticism and adds that it provides no prediction of unknown physical facts and only retrospectively projects new discoveries onto the text, exploiting the subtleties of the Arabic language (Hoodbhoy 1991: 67–69). In the book's Appendix, titled "They Call It Islamic Science," Hoodbhoy criticizes (indeed, ridicules) an international conference convened in Pakistan with governmental support and patronage in 1987, as well as articles published in a journal supported by the Pakistani scientific establishment around the same time; in both contexts, far-fetched ideas were promoted, such as "scientific" interpretations of Qur'anic verses and discussions of the composition of *jinn* (spirits), which a prominent atomic nuclear engineer suggested (in 1983) should be used as an energy source (Hoodbhoy 1991: 140–154). He sees Nasr as wanting to take science back to its premodern form (Hoodbhoy 1991: 69–74). Sardar's criticism of modern science does raise serious and valid

---

[29] Interestingly, Abdus Salam cited Bucaille to the effect that the Qur'an contains no passages incongruent with modern scientific information (Salam 1984: 180).

points, in his view, but those are not necessarily inspired by or related to religious considerations (Hoodbhoy 1991: 74–75). In sum, Hoodbhoy sees these thinkers' plans to Islamically reform science as ill-founded, ill-formulated, and ultimately worthless (Hoodbhoy 1991: 75).[30] It is worth noting that Sardar criticized Hoodbhoy (and Abdus Salam) as promoting a positivistic approach, whereby science ends up being guided by no ideals at all (see e.g., Sardar 1989: 134).

The book also dedicates considerable space to historical discussion. Hoodbhoy argues that major scientific figures in the Muslim world (Al-Kindi, Al-Razi, Ibn Sina, Ibn Rushd, Ibn Khaldun) were either "heretics" (that is, they entertained theological views that were deviant from official or mainstream ones) or had kept their religious ideas separate from their scientific work (Hoodbhoy 1991: 109-117). Since his 1991 monograph, Hoodbhoy has not published any substantial work on Islam and science; however, he has been engaged in science-related issues,[31] publicly denouncing pseudoscience as well as pedagogic and academic malpractice in Pakistan (see, for instance, Hoodbhoy 2015). In a 2017 interview, Hoodbhoy made the following strong statement: "Science resolutely refuses to take root in Muslim countries" (Bigliardi 2017b). He acknowledged that ideas about the Islamic reformation of science such as those advocated by Nasr and Sardar are subsiding. However, he showed concern about prominent politicians' support for pseudoscientific charlatans in Pakistan, as well as the diffusion of practices such as "faith healing" and a lack of acceptance of the theory of evolution among Muslims. Hoodbhoy pointed out that, while pseudoscience can be found everywhere, in Pakistan it is more difficult to "summon forces" against it. For this, he blamed several factors. First, the fact that science and religion are often unduly blended can lead to problematic practices, for instance granting extra points to students who have memorized the Qur'an, a practice which may mean access to positions of responsibility is granted to individuals with stronger credentials in religion than in science. Second, Hoodbhoy criticized the rote-learning pedagogy that is still prevalent in classrooms in the Muslim world. Third, there is a dearth of scientist role models in the Muslim world; the case of Abdus Salam, who was declared non-Muslim and hence forgotten, being a particularly painful example. Finally, Hoodbhoy exposed the widespread academic malpractice

---

[30] Hoodbhoy doesn't directly take up Al-Faruqi's ideas, but mentions Sardar's criticism of his views (Hoodbhoy 1991: 75). However, his criticism of Nasr and Sardar may generally apply to Al-Faruqi as well.

[31] He has contributed to scientific literacy in Pakistan, producing and anchoring the documentary series *Bazm-e-Kainat* (*Living in the Cosmos*, 1994) and *Asrar-e-Jahan* (*Mysteries of the Universe*, 2003).

across Pakistani universities such as the existence of "citation cartels" (formed with academics from various countries), who cite each other's papers in order to boost their rankings to levels that do not reflect their true merits.

Hoodbhoy thinks that the only way to achieve a peaceful relation between religion and science is to "put them into two separate, non-overlapping compartments. Leave science to scientists, to be pursued using scientific methods based on reason, logic, experiment and observation. And leave religion to the spiritual domain of the individual." He adds: "The only Muslim thinker who was able to successfully deal with this issue on the Indian subcontinent was Sayyid Ahmad Khan. Following the *mo'tazila* (rationalist) tradition, he insisted that one has to examine the etymology of the words in the Quran and then interpret and reinterpret until Islam ends up conforming with science." And he concludes: "This requires some terrific intellectual acrobatics, but there is really no other way" (Bigliardi 2017b).

The "New Generation"

Between the late 1990s and the early 2010s, a group of authors began marking a turn in the debates in Islam and modern science, contributing to it both academically and by reaching out to the general public and to educated nonspecialists. These authors were first studied by Stefano Bigliardi, who referred to them as a "new generation,"[32] in contrast to Bucaille, Al-Faruqi, Nasr, and Sardar's group. They include the Iranian physicist Mehdi Golshani (b. 1939), the Iraqi physicist and cosmologist Mohammad Basil Altaie (b. 1952), the French astrophysicist Bruno Abd-al-Haqq Guiderdoni (b. 1958), and the Algerian astrophysicist Nidhal Guessoum (b. 1960). They come from diverse cultural backgrounds; for instance, Golshani is a Shiite Muslim, and Guiderdoni is a convert. Most importantly, these authors by no means constitute a school of thought, and occasionally diverge significantly on some crucial topics, for instance the interpretation of supernatural miracles. It should also be remarked that this "new generation" is far from having overshadowed the "old" one, which remained influential, mostly through followers and successors, while the "new generation" was surfacing. The "new generation," however, did represent a conceptual shift, albeit initially slow and uncoordinated.

To start with, the professional background of all the authors in question is in the natural sciences; they are active as university professors and researchers. They do not advocate any reformation of the scientific method, much less its merging with the spiritual domain.[33] These thinkers downplay the relevance of

---

[32] See Bigliardi 2014a, later developed in Bigliardi 2014b and in Bigliardi 2014c.

[33] This is especially noteworthy for Guiderdoni, a self-professed Sufi practitioner. His position represents a shift in the perception of science within contemporary Sufism, one that has been appreciated by specialists in the field. See Piraino 2014.

the "scientific content" of the Qur'an, and in some cases utterly reject it. They are either partly or fully receptive to the concepts of Darwinian evolution, including human evolution, which they then interpret in a theistic vein. Finally, they do not claim that Islam is the only religion that can fully and consistently be harmonized with science; rather, they regard themselves as the representatives of a Muslim perspective in a global conversation on science and religion that includes other faiths, on a footing of equality. None of the authors of the older generation can be said to fully instantiate such traits. Other authors who satisfy such criteria but were not dealt with in Bigliardi's initial study include the Jordanian molecular biologist Rana Dajani (b. 1969) and the Algerian physicist Jamal Mimouni (b. 1956).[34]

Taner Edis: "Anti-Harmony"

Finally, and to complete the spectrum, the Turkish-American physicist Taner Edis (b. 1967), professor at Truman State University, published *An Illusion of Harmony. Science and Religion in Islam* (Edis 2007), for which Hoodbhoy wrote a laudatory blurb. Edis offers a systematic criticism of most of the theories about the harmony of Islam and science that we have summarized. He has also published books presenting critical discussions and rejections of religion (Edis 2002, 2008). Still, he encourages a nuanced and fair understanding of the contemporary Muslim world (Edis 2016). He also acknowledges that the West has its own "illusions of harmony" and clashes in the interaction of science and religion (Edis 2007: 239–251).

According to Edis, the notion of a "Golden Age" of science in Islam is in fact a "usable past," a myth based on historical oversimplifications and on a hasty juxtaposition of ancient and modern science (Edis 2007: 33–80). Needless to say, he is strongly critical of the *i'jaz* approach (Edis 2007: 94–100). In regard to Nasr, Edis is especially critical of his rejection of evolution, but he also considers Nasr's views on the necessity to prevent science from challenging a spiritual worldview as expressing a mindset that is ultimately hostile to science and leaves it no freedom. This, for Edis, is typical of "religious thinkers who have not made their peace with science" (Edis 2007: 206).

In his bold monograph, Edis raises multiple objections to modernist and liberal attempts at harmonizing Islam and science, pointing out, for instance, that traditional interpretations (such as the literal reading of supernatural narratives) sound less strained and are consequently more appealing to the public at large than liberal ones (Edis 2007: 219). Additionally, he notes that even liberal

---

[34] For a critical view of Bigliardi's discussion, see Azadegan 2014, and Bigliardi's response (Bigliardi 2014d).

views on Islam and science ultimately emphasize theological concepts like *tawhid* or ethical ones that are taken from sacred texts. However, this, in his view, inevitably causes clashes with the scientific enterprise, which should be unrestrained; for instance, an evolutionary biologist may deconstruct the concept of "altruistic" behavior, which a religious person may regard as part and parcel of a pious conduct (Edis 2007: 226–229).

Edis has expressed a critical appraisal, although cautious and respectful, of the position of the "new generation." He compares the group to the advocates of Islamic feminism, that is, to authors who defend feminist ideas by reinterpreting the Qur'an. Like Islamic feminists, Edis says, the above authors find themselves constrained by the fact that in most Muslim countries, "political imagination has become dominated by Islamist movements." Thus, Edis sees their approach as conservative in the sense that "the reinterpretations they propose are ways to update and preserve familiar conceptions of faith." Moreover, he sees the authors of this "new generation" as dangerously conflating "creative meaning-making with explanation" (Edis 2014).

To be sure, Edis does recognize the originality of the position of the "new generation" in comparison with that of other approaches. In particular, he points out, they are more sophisticated and scholarly than the advocates of *i'jaz* and creationists like Harun Yahya. However, he remarks that while being

> very sympathetic to ideas about divine design that might link up with biology or physical cosmology, they do not commit themselves to concrete claims that can be of use in a scientific context. Their notions of design remain vague, so that they do not risk being clearly wrong. ... Where explanations are concerned, they offer little of substance to criticize. (Edis 2014)

3 A Field(s)/Topical Map of the Debates

Modern science has produced a number of factual results and strong theories that have seriously challenged the traditional Islamic/religious conceptions of the world, life, humans, creation, ethics, and God's place in this new world. Most debates in Islam and the sciences fall into one of two categories: (a) theological issues, mainly God's place and role in the modern understanding of nature and the cosmos; (b) jurisprudential/ethical issues, that is, what should be allowed, on religious or ethical grounds, from the host of new possibilities that science has brought forth. Issues in the theological category include creation, naturalism, causality, miracles, evolution, randomness, and others. Issues in the jurisprudential/ethical category include biomedical acts, for example, surrogacy, organ donation, euthanasia, cloning, and so on. New issues with ethical dimensions, such as artificial intelligence, transhumanism, and so on, will be considered in the next section.

While many of the topics of the jurisprudential/ethical type are novel (though some analogies with premodern cases can be and have been drawn for some of them), several of the theological topics are not new. The question of creation is very old, predating Islam and the monotheistic religions. Even when one accepts the idea of a creator for the world/cosmos, one may still ask: when and how did/does He create (from nothing or from pre-existing disordered material, using some preset rules/laws, etc.)? Likewise, the concept of causality (the same effects will always result from given factors, i.e., A will always lead to B) has been a key issue for Islamic and other philosophers and theologians (recall Al-Ghazali's stance and Ibn Rushd's response a century later). However, modern science has added fuel to the debates by introducing probability into many phenomena, indeterminism (in quantum effects, in chaos, and such), and randomness. Modern science has also fanned the flames of debate with the theory of evolution, explaining the history of life in a "natural way," without recourse to a creator. And if that were not enough, modern science – even when it accepts people's belief in a creator, as long as He is not invoked to explain natural phenomena – flatly reject "miracles," at least when understood as violations or suspensions of the laws of nature.

Let us briefly review some of the above issues; many will be covered in detail in future Elements in this series, and some will resurface later in this Element.

Theological Issues

Naturalism

The *Oxford Languages Dictionary* defines "naturalism" as the philosophical belief that all phenomena result from natural causes and properties, thus excluding supernatural explanations. Furthermore, "naturalism" is usually divided into "methodological naturalism" and "philosophical naturalism." The former is a principle that excludes supernatural agents from scientific explanations of phenomena in nature but is silent on any belief in "noninterfering" supernatural entities. Philosophical naturalism is the rejection of the existence of any supernatural entities (God, spirits, angels, etc.) or beliefs (life after death, divine revelation or inspiration, etc.), whether they interfere with natural processes or not; this is tantamount to materialism and atheism.

Modern science strongly insists on methodological naturalism, and many scientists adopt philosophical naturalism; that is, they are atheists/materialists. This has led many Muslims to perceive modern science as inherently nontheistic, as keeping God out of the picture or "tying God's hands" (as Nasr has put it), and thus to reject methodological naturalism. Indeed, some thinkers insist that God does act in nature, for example by producing earthquakes as punishment for those who have sinned and deserve such punishment. Most Muslim scientists (or, more accurately, natural philosophers) of the Golden Age, however, implicitly adopted methodological naturalism in their study of nature, as they always attempted to explain phenomena using only natural causes, never invoking any supernatural agents. Many Muslim thinkers, from Ibn Rushd to Sayyid Ahmad Khan, have underscored the regularity that God has put in the world (God's "covenant", "faithfulness", and "consistency"), without which we cannot make predictions, nor even trust any knowledge we accumulate.

Divine Action

Does God act in any way in the world if, according to science, all phenomena in that world have natural explanations? Muslims often insist that believing that God does not act directly in physical phenomena but only through the laws of nature is equivalent to *deism* (i.e., the idea that God created the universe and then let it run on its own). Many thinkers distinguish between "direct" and "indirect" divine action (Draper 2005: 281), the former being where God "acts outside of the ordinary course of nature," and the latter being where God "uses natural causes to bring about an effect." Thinkers also make the distinction between "General Divine Action" (GDA) and "Special Divine Action" (SDA), the former being God's general "sustaining" of the universe (laws and phenomena only working through His presence and permission), and the latter representing actions at specific points/moments, whether directly (intervening, suspending the normal laws) or "indirectly" (using "openings" in the laws of nature).[35] We should note that SDA has elicited critiques that it suggests capriciousness or uncaringness on the part of God (cf. Wiles 1999: 16–17).

Searching for ways in which God could act using natural means, observers have long noted that the indeterminism of quantum mechanics (in its standard form) could be a way in which God acts in nature, since one would normally assume that He (the Omniscient and Omnipotent) is able to set the outcome of the "wave function collapse process" to any preferred choice from among those that the laws of physics allow. God could then "steer" events in one direction or another, provided that He acts on each and every particle/atom/molecule in a "coordinated" manner.

The second proposal of physical divine action is through nonlinear processes that lead to chaos: tiny effects in the initial conditions of a system, whether microscopic or macroscopic, leading to hugely amplified results. Here again, since tiny interventions and changes are essentially impossible to notice, God

---

[35] For detailed discussions of various ways to consider GDA and SDA, particularly the latter, see Saunders 2002.

could take such an approach in His actions. A good application of this effect would be the parting of the Red Sea by the "strong east wind" (the Bible's words). However, this would also be grounds for believing in God's intervention in natural catastrophes, which many lay people believe are God's punishing acts, but this viewpoint raises various concerns.

On the Muslim side, there have been very few, if any, fully argued proposals about God's action in the world, perhaps due to the high level of sensitivity surrounding this issue. One article that has tackled the subject is Abdelhakim Al-Khalifi's "Divine Action between Necessity and Choice" (Al-Khalifi 1998), which explores the views of key classical philosophers (Al-Farabi and Ibn Sina) and theological schools of Islam (Mu'tazilism and Ash'arism). Al-Khalifi contrasts the Ash'arites' views that God's action is totally free and unconstrained with the Mu'tazilites' position that God's act of creation was free but that God has constrained Himself to being just and good and rewarding/punishing those who follow/disobey His divine directives to us to be just and good.

Indeed, the Islamic heritage can be constructively tapped into; for instance, the old "rationalist" Mu'tazilite theology, which insists on the concept of divine laws, could be revived to help resolve this area of tension. Similarly, M. Basil Altaie has found some richness and fruitfulness in Al-Ghazali's views that could be exploited (see Bigliardi 2014b: 72–76), and it would be very useful to see those ideas unpacked (using Al-Ghazali or other sources). Finally, another approach consists in the Sufi conception of the world as being a divine effusion; if everything is (in some way) "within" God, then divine action becomes a given.

Guessoum has suggested an alternative viewpoint (Guessoum 2016a): that God acts only on minds/spirits. The "spirit" is sometimes, but not always, identified with the "mind," which is itself rather abstractly defined as the ensemble of mental processes (reasoning, perception, consciousness, etc.). The spirit tends to have a religious connotation, being associated with religious activity, including perception of and perhaps communication with God. In the Islamic tradition, the general understanding is that the spirit is not only the connection and communication channel between humans and God but also the fundamental "driving force" that God infused in humans. More recently, with debates of reductionism in relation to mind and consciousness, the idea that a top-down causation from mind/spirit to the brain, leading from ideas to physical acts which carry on into nature, has become more acceptable. Cosmologist George Ellis has also supported this approach (Ellis 1995), adding that top-down causation from mind/spirit to the brain could be envisioned via the aforementioned quantum processes. And finally, philosopher Philip Clayton has adopted and expounded upon the idea of divine action through human influence or mental causation via the spirit (Clayton 2008).

Miracles

Miracles constitute one of the most contentious issues in the debates on religion and science. Miracles are not as fundamental to some religions as to others, but in their direct connection to the more important issue of divine action in the world, they are essential to address. One must start with basic questions that seek to define miracles and delineate the extent of their manifestation: (1) Are miracles violations of the laws of nature, or are they simply striking events that are scientifically improbable? (2) Do miracles occur only through the hands of prophets or also those of saints and even ordinary people (today)? (3) Did the Prophet Muhammad perform physical miracles? (4) How is one to understand the "miracles" that the Qur'an attributes to other prophets (Abraham, Moses, Jesus)?

The question of miracles cannot be addressed without reference to modern science. One must consider concepts and issues such as causality and determinism, and principles such as the conservation of energy and electric charge, and so on. In the Islamic tradition, one must first recall that the term "miracle" (*mu'jiza*) does not occur in the Qur'an. Rather the term *ayah*, or sign, is used every time an event or phenomenon is described, always implying God's omnipotence and humans' limitedness (e.g., Q 29:22, 35:44). *Ayah* is used in the Qur'an to refer to both extraordinary and regular phenomena in nature around us as well as to the verses of the Qur'an itself, all of which are meant to direct us to God.

In modern times, several famous Muslim scholars and thinkers have adopted rationalistic or even naturalistic views with regard to the "classical" miracles. Abduh's modernist exegesis of the Qur'an included naturalistic explanations for events that had usually been considered direct interventions by God. Sayyid Ahmad Khan rejected the idea that miracles violated natural laws. Muhammad Asad's commentary[36] on the Qur'an coherently included rationalistic reinterpretations of "miracles" (e.g., the Prophet's night journey from Mecca to Jerusalem and ascent to heaven, etc.). Recently, a few Muslim thinkers have also expressed interesting views on the subject.

Golshani considers "miracles" as events that fall under different laws to those we know of as the laws of nature, or a combination of laws (such as a magnetic field canceling out gravity and making an object float in the air, in the example he gives). There is no violation of the laws of nature. However, even though Golshani regards miracles as not central to religiosity, he does not advocate metaphorical interpretations of any of the Qur'anic miracle stories, but rather keeps open the possibility of

---

[36] Muhammad Asad (1900–1992), a Central European convert to Islam, had an active and rich life, lived between Europe, the Arabian Peninsula, and India/Pakistan, and wrote some well-received books, including an English translation and commentary on the Qur'an, *The Message of the Qur'an* (1980). He combined deep faith with an analytical, rational approach to Islam.

future explanations being provided when new knowledge about nature is discovered (Bigliardi 2013; 2014b: 57–60).

A similar view is adopted by Altaie, who first insists that "God does not rule this world miraculously but according to well-defined laws," but further stresses that the quantum world has shown that extraordinary events (a person going through a door without opening it, in the example he gives) can happen albeit exceedingly rarely. He thus considers miracles as extremely rare events that occur within the laws of nature, even though in some cases we may not yet have the knowledge to explain them (Bigliardi 2014b: 81).

Bruno Abd-al-Haqq Guiderdoni distinguishes between "divine providence" – that is, extraordinary coincidences that violate no laws and which Muslims consider as divine "intervention"; "small miracles," so to speak – and the events that are described in the Qur'an as apparently supernatural (e.g., a clay bird coming to life and flying off) and which he proposes should be interpreted spiritually. For instance, the famous splitting of the moon he interprets as "the splitting of the heart of the believer," the unveiling of the secrets hidden in one's heart on Doomsday. He insists that "the laws of nature are constantly valid" because thinking of God as acting here and there simply "lowers our idea of God" (Bigliardi 2014b: 145–146).[37]

Evolution

The debates around evolution and Islam have not subsided in recent years. On the contrary, Muslim rejectionists of evolution have continued to promote their views, essentially by adopting and translating American creationist or intelligent-design arguments, though often without explicit attribution. Perhaps the biggest "star" of Arab-Muslim creationism today is Eyad Qunaibi (b. 1975), a Jordanian professor of pharmacology who, while having published nothing on evolution (according to his ResearchGate page[38]), has produced dozens of videos against the theory on his YouTube channel,[39] which has over 1 million subscribers. Qunaibi rejects (macro) evolution completely and presents "scientific" and other arguments against it.

However, we have recently witnessed a new trend: the appearance of a new "human-exception" type of creationism. Proponents of such proposals include David Solomon Jalajel (Jalajel 2009, 2018), Nazir Khan and Yasir Qadhi (Khan and Qadhi 2018), and others. These authors attempt to elaborate scenarios whereby the distinct creation of Adam is preserved, humanity is unique and special, "Muslim orthodoxy"[40] is upheld, whatever fits with this in the theory of evolution is

---

[37] For a discussion of miracles inspired by Al-Ghazali, Averroes, and Nursi, but also David Hume (1711–1776) and Charles Sanders Peirce (1839–1914), see Yazicioglu 2013.

[38] Eyad Qunaibi's ResearchGate profile: www.researchgate.net/profile/Eyad-Qunaibi.

[39] Eyad Qunaibi's YouTube channel: www.youtube.com/c/eyadqunaibi.

[40] As Jalajel himself refers to it.

adopted,[41] and anything else is rejected. For instance, Jalajel writes: "The following is apparent from the textual evidence: Adam was created by God directly from earth. Both Adam and his wife were created by God without the agency of parents" (Jalajel 2009: 49). He and other authors with this approach accept, uphold, and insist on Adam having been sixty cubits (almost 30 meters) of height (as in a famous *hadith*). To insist that Adam was created *separately*, even if one claims to accept later human evolution, is definitely creationism (Guessoum 2011), even if some authors (Malik 2020: 251–254) try to deny this association; indeed, the new approach seems to try to avoid association with creationism by accepting some aspects of evolution and coming up with scenarios, often far-fetched, that include a special creation of Adam.

Khan and Qadhi insist that the creation of Adam is a matter of the "unseen"; they write: "No human being can go back in time and determine precisely what happened at the time of Adam and Eve, and thus it constitutes something empirically unobservable, a matter of the unseen (*ghayb*)" (Khan & Qadhi 2018). This is simply wrong: today we can retrace humans genetically by following mutations and by dating back the (now) very rich fossil record. These authors want to negate science's ability to explore the past and produce reliable evidence by distinguishing between empirical sciences, which can provide us with direct evidence, and historical sciences, which only produce indirect evidence. This is simplistic and misleading, however, as both geology and astronomy are physical sciences, and yet they explore the past and produce reliable evidence from multiple, intersecting, and mutually confirming methods.

On the proevolution side, recent contributions include Guessoum's chapter on "Islam and Evolution" in his 2010 book; Adnan Ibrahim's thirty-episode video series[42] promoting a harmonious view of Islam and evolution (2014); Guessoum's "Islamic Theological Views on Darwinian Evolution" (Guessoum 2016b); and Caner Taslaman's book chapter "Can a Muslim Be an Evolutionist?" (Taslaman 2022). One noteworthy "external" review and analysis of the "Islam and evolution" debates is Damian Howard's *Being Human in Islam: The Impact of the Evolutionary Worldview* (Howard 2011).

Jurisprudential and Ethical Issues

Discussions of genetic engineering, cloning, stem-cell research and their applications have become commonplace in the world, including in Islamic societies, particularly with the advent of CRISPR-Cas9, the versatile and powerful

---

[41] "Islam can accommodate the claim that God created the many species of animal and plant life on Earth though gradual stages" (Jalajel 2009: 149).

[42] Adnan Ibrahim, "The Evolution Series", YouTube, https://www.youtube.com/playlist?list=PLD-NW5zvOeHT6HHTeXB0723jIwaea2xPD, accessed January 14, 2023.

gene-editing technique. We now have to address much more challenging topics such as "gene drives" (systematically removing a "bad" gene from an entire species), "synthetic life"[43] (sometimes referred to as "artificial life"), technologically modified, "augmented," or "enhanced" humans[44] (sometimes referred to as "transhumanism"), and even "immortality."[45] The definition of "life" itself is being seriously affected by these changes, with implications for beginning-of-life and end-of-life issues (from conception to euthanasia), as we shall see below.

Muslim jurists, philosophers, and scientists have been contending with these developments, using Islamic principles such as the "preservation of life," the preservation of "lineage," the sanctity and dignity of the human body and mind, and so on (e.g. Woodman et al. 2019). More generally, the idea of "playing God" is often invoked to express general objections to such manipulations. The above bio-interventions raise a host of ethical and/or religious questions, including the following: When should editing human or animal genomes be allowed? How does one define "bad genes"? Where do we draw the line between "fixing" flaws and "enhancing" bodies, particularly brains? What about unintended consequences? Should cloning be allowed, for humans or for animals? What are the moral concerns? The field of Islamic bioethics has matured substantially in recent times, with the appearance of numerous papers, books, conferences, projects, and encyclopedias (e.g. Ghaly 2013; Padela 2021).

Surrogacy

Surrogacy is an issue that has been discussed for several decades now (for a review, see Matthews 2021) but has been revisited due to advances in science, particularly genetics. In 1986, the the Fiqh Council of the Muslim World League, and the Fiqh Council of the Organization of the Islamic Conference both issued rulings permitting surrogacy for married couples or between "co-wives," that is, wives of the same husband, for example, if one is unable to carry through a pregnancy while another one can (Matthews 2021). Soon, however, this second possibility was denied by the Fiqh councils for fear of lineage confusion (but it was accepted by some independent

---

[43] For discussions of "synthetic life" and ethics, see for instance, Cho and Relman 2010 and Craig Venter's 2010 TED talk, "Watch Me Unveil 'Synthetic Life'" (www.ted.com/talks/craig_venter_watch_me_unveil_synthetic_life).

[44] See, for instance, the "Augmented Human International Conferences Series" (www.augmented-human.com/), running since 2010; also the report of the workshop on "Human Enhancement and the Future of Work" of the Royal Society, the Academy of Medical Sciences, the British Academy, and the Royal Academy of Engineering (March 2012; http://royalsociety.org/policy/projects/human-enhancement/workshop-report/).

[45] See the project on "The Science, Philosophy, and Theology of Immortality" (www.sptimmortalityproject.org/) at the University of California, Riverside.

scholars,[46] by analogy to "wet-nursing"). The example given was that of a woman who becomes pregnant by normal sexual relations with her husband, but around the same time decides to be a surrogate for her husband's other wife; Muslim jurists thought it might be difficult to tell who the baby belongs/is related to upon delivery; thus, surrogacy should not be allowed even between co-wives. Needless to say, DNA analysis can easily solve this "confusion," thus science negates this argument against surrogacy.

However, Islamic jurists have advanced more general arguments opposing any surrogacy under any circumstances (such as helping a couple procreate and thus achieve greater happiness). Islamic scholars have cited Qur'anic verses that seem to indicate that progeny is supposed to come only from couples; for instance: "And Allah has made for you spouses from among yourselves, and has given you sons and grandchildren from your spouses, and has given you of the good things" (16:72), underlining the statement "sons and grandchildren from your spouses." However, surrogacy does preserve the genetic affiliation of (both) the "donor" man and woman; the pregnancy of the surrogate mother does not affect this. Another argument used against surrogacy is that, in some places around the world, it is conducted for a fee, and this implies some form of exploitation of the surrogate mother's poverty and financial needs. Finally, the traditionalists say that there is nothing in the entire body of classical Islamic jurisprudence (*hadith*, analog case, or opinion) to support surrogacy. However, this just demonstrates that science (and medical technology) has brought something new and challenging for Islamic biomedical discussions; looking back at medieval references will not always solve a (new) problem.

Organ Donation

Organ donation has been a fixture of Islamic (and other legal) biomedical ethical discussions and rulings ever since it became a possible intervention that could save or at least greatly improve the life of a patient with a highly deficient organ.[47] Muslim jurists often approach this issue from the perspective of the principle of *maslaha* (common interest). The topic has seen a resurgence of interest among bioethicists, including Muslim scholars, as the definition of (or criterion for) "death" has become much more complicated than had previously

---

[46] Scholars who accept gestational surrogacy include Dr. Na'eem Yaaseen (Ahmad 2006: 242).

[47] Medical anthropologist Sherine Hamdy reconstructed the debate on organ transplants in Egypt in the late 1990s. Diverging religious views were offered respectively by the Grand Sheik of Al Azhar Muhammad Sayyid Tantawy (1928–2010) and Sheik Mohammed Metwali Al-Sha'rawi (1911–1998). The former condoned the practice (under strict conditions), defining it as altruistic; the latter spoke against it, arguing that organs, as they are not owned by human beings, cannot be donated (Hamdy 2008).

been assumed. With "resuscitation" now regularly being achieved for patients whose hearts and respiration have stopped for hours, and even those whose brains have sent no signals for a long period, death is not what it used to be. In a nutshell, "death" is not considered a moment anymore (the "moment of death"), but rather a *process*, starting with the stoppage of the heart and ending when brain cells have deteriorated to the point that they can no longer resume their functions of sending and receiving signals inside the brain and to and from various organs. In some cases, the brain is considered "dead," but medical instruments can keep the heart, lungs, and other organs functioning.

With this significant paradigm shift in medicine, the questions of when and under what conditions organ transplants can be authorized have required renewed discussion. Neurologist M. Y. Rady and biomedical ethicist J. L. Verheijde write: "International Muslim scholars should reevaluate previous Islamic rulings[48] and provide guidance about current practice of end-of-life organ donation" (Rady and Verheijde 2009: 882). These authors insist that the important questions to be asked here are at what point the removal of an organ can be permitted and, at least as importantly, whether the removal of an organ during the death process affects the latter. Moreover, they add, there should be at least as much emphasis on the donor as on the person receiving the organ.

Euthanasia

Euthanasia, from the Greek for "good death" or "easy death," has become a topic of wide discussion in recent years, partly because some countries have legislated for this act, allowing it under certain conditions, and partly because some doctors – most famously the American Dr. Jack Kevorkian (1928–2011), labeled "Doctor Death" – have practiced euthanasia with numerous suffering patients who saw no prospects of recovery and thus wanted to die. Euthanasia is thus often referred to as "mercy killing." Islam, and other religions and ethical systems, have been faced with the question of how to deal with this relatively new practice. What principles are brought to bear on the matter?

First, the fact that a patient wants to die is not considered a valid argument for Muslim jurists, since Islam strongly abhors and outlaws suicide. Its punishment is eternal hell; in fact, whoever commits this act is denied a proper funeral

---

[48] Major Islamic rulings on organ donation, which include "definitions" of death, include the Organization of the Islamic Conference (now: Organization of Islamic Cooperation) Fiqh Academy's 1986 *fatwa*; the Muslim World League's Fiqh Academy's 1987 ruling; the Islamic Jurisprudence Assembly Council (Saudi Arabia) in 1988; the *fatwa* by Al-Azhar University (Cairo) in 2009 (allowing organ donation from a "recently deceased" person if consent had been given before death); the Fiqh Council of North America (FCNA)'s ruling in 2018 (rejecting brain death and only permitting organ donation after the cardiac death of the donor).

service. Secondly, human life is not only sacred, it is God's property and prerogative; no one is allowed to interfere with His will and authority over when it should end, the date and time of death (*ajal*) being known to God alone. Endurance of one's pain must thus be accepted; it is highly rewarded in the afterlife.

Consequently, essentially all Muslim scholars (from Saudi Arabia's late Grand Mufti Bin Baz to Iran's Ayatollah Khamenei) reject euthanasia. In 2005, the famous and influential Egyptian/Qatari Islamic scholar Yusuf Al-Qaradawi (1926-2022) rejected "mercy killing," only allowing medication to be stopped if it "proves to be of no use,"[49] when the sickness "gets out of hand." He added: "the physician can practice this for the sake of the patient's comfort and the relief of his family." The Iranian researchers Kiarash Aramesh and Heydar Shadi point to two instances where "passive assistance in allowing a terminally ill patient to die" would be permissible under Islamic law: (a) "administering analgesic agents that might shorten the patient's life, with the purpose of relieving the physical pain or mental distress"; and (b) "withdrawing futile treatment on the basis of informed consent (of the immediate family members who act on the professional advice of the physicians in charge of the case), allowing death to take its natural course" (Aramesh and Shadi 2007).

Cloning

Cloning became both a household word and a headache for ethicists and religious scholars around the world when the sheep Dolly was cloned in 1996, and the prospect of human cloning appeared on the horizon.

Cloning can be of one of two types: *reproductive*, where a copy of an animal (or potentially a person) is produced with a genome identical to the original one (this is what people commonly think of when "cloning" is mentioned), or *therapeutic*, where an embryo (again identical) is produced in order to harvest stem cells that can then be used to either perform medical studies (say the search for a cure to a given disease) or for the production of a specific organ to replace a defective one. Muslim jurists unanimously reject reproductive cloning, considering it a form of "playing God" and a disruption of lineage and dignity, not to mention their concern about the technique's potential dangers, with the possible creation of severe abnormalities. The technique is also banned in dozens of countries, though some advocates of the practice are racing against time to make it a *fait accompli*.[50]

---

[49] See forum discussion on IslamOnline.Net, March 22, 2005, https://web.archive.org/web/20110222114112/http:/www.islamonline.net/servlet/Satellite?pagename= IslamOnline-English-Ask_Scholar/FatwaE/FatwaE&cid=1119503544774.

[50] "Human Cloning Policies," Center for Genetics and Society, n.d., www.geneticsandsociety.org/internal-content/human-cloning-policies.

Therapeutic cloning is more open to debate among Muslim scholars and in the rest of the world. It is allowed in Japan, the UK, and several Muslim countries: Iran, Qatar, and Saudi Arabia (and probably in other Muslim-majority countries too, though information is scarce, highlighting the need for more research), under certain conditions, for instance with the exclusion of commercial usage. There is no evidence to date that this technique has been used anywhere,[51] though this may well change soon. This is another case in which science (and its subsequent applications) has shaken up religious circles, forcing them to understand new breakthroughs and techniques and consider general ethical and religious principles and how they can be applied to the problems of today and tomorrow.

Concluding Remarks

Numerous issues and topics at the intersection of Islam and the sciences require careful study and debate. They range widely from the theophilosophical (e.g. naturalism and divine action, evolution, etc.) to the very practical, ethical, and jurisprudential (e.g. organ donation, surrogacy, euthanasia, etc.). Many of these topics have long been discussed by Muslim theologians, jurists, and philosophers, some for hundreds of years. However, science, with its continuous and accelerating progress, keeps bringing new grist to the mill. Muslim scholars have started to realize that in order to address these topics in an informed and meaningful way, one must not simply rely on old Islamic principles, however general they may be, nor address topics in piecemeal or reactive ways, but rather consider more holistic and general paradigms, that is, address issues in a framework of the meaning, purpose, and value of life (human and other) as well as humans' place in the universe. There is growing awareness of the need to construct a framework[52] (something that can be described as "Holistic Islamic ethics," for instance) for thinking about newly emerging science-related issues and producing coherent ideas on the various topics that do or will need some treatment.

4 The New and Future Islam and Science Debates

The ancient and modern debates that we have summarized set a rich and complex agenda for the interaction of Islam and science and continue to be the object of intense discussion among Muslim authors, as well as of meticulous

---

[51] "Cloning Fact Sheet," National Human Genome Research Institute, n.d., www.genome.gov/about-genomics/fact-sheets/Cloning-Fact-Sheet.

[52] See, for example, the agenda and program of the Research Center for Islamic Legislation and Ethics (CILE)'s Medicine & Bioethics department: www.cilecenter.org/area-research/medicine-bioethics.

study by historians of ideas. New topics, however, keep coming to the fore. Emerging debates are fueled by recent scientific research that pushes for a revision of old questions or calls for novel theorization. Additionally, high-speed and deep-impact technological change opens up possibilities which only a few years ago seemed confined to the realm of science fiction or even dystopia. And though these research developments are ongoing and far from settled (scientifically and technically), the resulting scenarios are accompanied by ethical or theological challenges. Let us explore a few examples.

Fine-Tuning, the Multiverse, and Pre–Big Bang Cosmology

Cosmology and Islam is a topic that has been discussed at length by many authors, for a variety of reasons: (a) many verses of the Qur'an (and to a lesser degree the Prophet's *hadiths*) lend themselves to cosmological discussion; (b) in the classical/medieval era of the Islamic civilization, cosmology was the subject of a number of interesting doctrines, some closer to astronomy and others to mysticism, theology, or philosophy; and (c) modern cosmology has brought fresh and sometimes challenging ideas to the field (such as fine-tuning, the multiverse, and pre–big bang theories) and have thus led to renewed interest in it. One forthcoming Element will be devoted to all these aspects, from Qur'anic exegesis related to cosmology to classical Islamic cosmological doctrines, all the way to modern theories. Here we shall limit ourselves to the new and future debates around cosmology and Islam, namely fine-tuning, the multiverse, and pre–big bang proposals.

Fine-tuning is the realization, which science has come to over the last half-century, that our universe has just the right laws, parameters, and building blocks to allow for complexity, life, intelligence, and conscious-ness to arise. On the one hand, there was no obvious reason why those laws and parameters had to have those features; on the other hand, if that were not the case, we would not be here to discuss them. So is this an obvious and trivial fact, or is it remarkable?[53] And if so, what explanation can be given for it? As could have been predicted, Muslim thinkers[54] have found in this another manifestation of "design," here at a cosmic scale, and related it to the Creator and the purpose of creation, as have theists from other religions, particularly monotheistic ones. This is an ongoing debate,[55] and here we restrict ourselves to pointing out the relatively new ideas brought forward by the American philosopher Robin Collins on fine-tuning and discoverability (Collins 2016, 2018).

---

[53] An excellent recent review of the topic is Lewis and Barnes 2016.
[54] See Guessoum 2010: Chapter 10; Khokhar 2018.
[55] See, for instance, Doko 2019.

The concept of the multiverse has been the subject of extensive work, both scientifically and philosophically; it too is a topic that goes back centuries if not millennia, if one considers the "many-worlds" debates of ancient and medieval times to very similar to, or possibly the same as, the multiverse debates of today. The latter are fueled by science (fine-tuning, eternal inflation, bubble universes, many-worlds interpretation of quantum mechanics, etc.), while earlier debates were based on philosophical arguments. Today's multiverse is partly a response to the fine-tuning problem and partly a result of (as-yet-unconfirmed) models/theories that predict the (possible) existence of countless universes of very different laws and parameters; the existence of one bio-friendly universe is then not only unsurprising but is even to be expected.

Some Muslim thinkers have resisted the multiverse idea, regarding it as the materialists' response to cosmic fine-tuning, which theists see as a sign of divine design. Others have welcomed it, considering it a sign of God's omnipotence,[56] and recalling the fact that a number of illustrious Muslim thinkers of the past supported the "many-worlds" idea. Indeed, the great philosopher Al-Farabi (ca. 872–ca. 950) promoted it, and Ibn Sina (980–1037) accepted it, either as "worlds" within "our world" or outside of it; the same goes for the polymath Al-Biruni (973–1050) and the theologian and exegetist Fakhr Al-Din Al-Razi (1150–1210), both of whom mainly argued that God's grace and creation are infinite in time and space. The prime opponent of the "many-worlds" doctrine was Al-Ghazali (1058–1111), who considered our world as the single best possible one. In recent times, some Muslim scientists and thinkers have expressed various views on the multiverse. The astrophysicist Jamal Mimouni abhors the idea: "From an ontological point of view," he states, "it's a catastrophe, because you're proposing things you can never observe, universes that are causally disconnected from our universe" (El-Showk 2016).

Pre–big bang models are based on the possibility that the universe did not emerge from "nothing." In particular, if its internal mass-energy is large enough, then it will (in hundreds of billions of years) collapse back on itself under its own gravity (in a "big crunch" event); however, it will not disappear into "nothingness," but rather produce a new universe, perhaps with somewhat different laws and parameters.[57] One could then consider pre–big bang phases on the basis of "quantum gravity," a theory which remains elusive. Moreover, the physicist Martin Bojowald (2007) warns that

---

[56] "It is Allah Who has created seven heavens and of the earth the like thereof (i.e., seven)" ("seven" being commonly interpreted as "many") – Q 65:12.

[57] Altaie has argued for a bouncing universe, which he views as consistent with the Qur'an. He stated: "We found a possibility for a flat universe to go through a collapse phase, a Big Crunch, before bouncing back to a new creation" (El-Showk 2016).

extrapolations to "before" the big bang (before any "rebirth" from a previous collapse) "require exceedingly precise knowledge of the present state [of the universe] that cannot realistically be obtained." In other words, "scientific" discussions of "before the big bang" are, and will long remain, largely speculative. This has not prevented scores of articles being written on this subject, reviving old debates of the eternal versus finite-age universe, a highly controversial debate among classical Muslim thinkers, philosophers and theologians.

Consciousness

Consciousness is the general state of being awake and aware of what is happening around us. Self-consciousness, more complex and challenging to explain, is one's awareness of one's own existence, sensations, thoughts, intentions, decision-making, and so on. How self-consciousness (in particular) arises, how it relates to reason, how much complexity (in the brain) it requires, which animals have it, and whether we can construct a "collective" self-consciousness, and so on, are all parts of what has been called "the hard problem." In the West, and in relation to psychology and (now) neuroscience, consciousness has been the subject of investigation and discussion for centuries. In philosophy (of mind) and psychology, the above features of (subjective) experience of thoughts, feelings, decision-making processes, and the like have been referred to as "qualia" (plural of "quale"). How these relate to the physical world, both inside and outside the brain, has been the subject of intense studies. Theories of consciousness are often divided into "physicalist" and "non-/anti-physicalist," or "reductive" and "nonreductive" approaches. Physicalist or reductive theories attempt to explain qualia in terms of physical, chemical, and biological (neurological) processes in the brain. Nonphysicalist or nonreductive varieties invoke either emergent phenomena[58] or nonphysical, dualist types of consideration.

Islamic thinkers tend to emphasize the "conscious of one's existence" part of consciousness and link that to human nature (and how it is unique and different from that of, say, animals[59]), intrinsic faith (*fitrah*), its relation to the spirit or soul, and to our special place and purpose on Earth (*khalifah*, God's vicegerent).

---

[58] Emergence (in science) refers to the fact that systems of greater complexity exhibit new properties or phenomena that could not exist if the system was simpler. For instance, atoms cannot individually perform various cell functions, and these cannot do what organs do (e.g., pump blood), which then combine in animals in complex ways, and so on.

[59] Insistence is made on man's "special" creation, when God breathed into him from His soul, when He taught Adam the "names" and challenged the angels to match his capacity but they failed to do so, and the like.

For instance, Turkish neuropsychologist Nevzat Tarhan writes: "Man is a being that adds meaning to everything and that is aware of his existence. Consciousness is one of the properties that distinguishes man from the other living beings and the most important and distinct property forming the difference that distinguishes him from the other species. Consciousness is a step between spirit and body" (Tarhan 2012).

In Islamic literature, consciousness is simply related to being awake or asleep; in the latter state, one completely loses awareness of one's surroundings and even of one's existence. Furthermore, several verses in the Qur'an refer to sleep as a "temporary" death; for instance: "And it is He who takes your souls at night (in sleep), and He knows what you commit in the day, then He raises you up therein to complete your appointed term" (6:60). Thus, Muslim writers often refer to sleep, where consciousness is lost, as a "small death," hence consciousness is related to the spirit or soul, which (in a dualistic conception) can be separated from the body in a temporary or permanent act. Sufi-inclined thinkers, however, consider consciousness as permeating the cosmos (panpsychism), and as not being limited to humans. A representative of this approach is Mohammed Rustom who, in his article "The Great Chain of Consciousness" (Rustom 2017), asks (rhetorically) "Do all things possess awareness?" He uses Sufi terms for consciousness (*wijdan*, instead of the usual word *wa'y*) and links it to *wujud* (existence or finding) to define consciousness as "finding God in ecstasy," as per Ibn Arabi (d. 1240), perhaps the greatest master of Sufism ever. Rustom then explains, again in a Sufi vision, that all things and phenomena, including inanimate ones, are "modes of God's consciousness" (God being "pure consciousness"). Finally, a jump is made from the claim that "things are modes of God's consciousness or self-awareness" to the assumption that all things have some level or amount of consciousness or self-awareness (which is measured by "how intense they are on the scale of consciousness"). Thus, the old "great chain of being"[60] is replaced by "the great chain of consciousness." Rustom finds justification for this in the Qur'anic verse: "And unto God prostrates whosoever is in the heavens and the earth, willingly or unwillingly" (57:1). He likes panpsychism as a "single explanatory fact that unites our seemingly disparate parts of reality because it extends consciousness beyond the organisms in the brain to all other seemingly 'inert' forms of matter." He takes this further: "That many if not most Muslim metaphysicians view all things, even seemingly inanimate ones, as alive should be taken quite literally." For him, all

---

[60] A hierarchical structure of all matter and life (God, angels, humans, animals, plants, minerals) that was widely adopted by medieval thinkers, Christians and Muslims.

things in the cosmos, from particles to galaxies, are living beings. His justification is from Ibn Arabi who insisted that

> The name Alive [*al-Ḥayy*] is an essential name of God – glory be to Him! Therefore, nothing can emerge from Him but living things. Hence, all of the cosmos is alive, for indeed the nonexistence of life, or the existence in the cosmos of an existent thing that is not alive, has no divine support, whereas every contingent thing must have a support. So, what you consider to be inanimate is in fact alive. (Ibn ʿArabi, in his *Futūḥāt*, as cited, with slight editing, by Rustom 2017)

Finally, Rustom hails panpsychism for its environmental benefits: "If, for example, we believe a tree has consciousness, not just biological life, and that it participates in the same awareness, being, life, and consciousness as humans, we would likely feel more responsible about our custodianship over it" (Rustom 2017).

Free Will

Free will, that is, the human ability to make choices and responsible decisions without external coercion and its relation to divine decree, action, and destiny, has been a major issue of discussion among philosophers and theologians since ancient times. Modern science has brought additional information to the debate in the form of experiments and physical processes as well as principles such as causal connections, determinism, and emergence. In Islam, the debates on free will have been fierce, even dividing major theological schools.

The Qur'an seems to argue both ways: for God's decree and predestination of people's faith, on the one hand, and for man's freedom of belief and action and responsibility over one's acts, on the other. Verse 14:4 states: "then God leads astray whomsoever He will, and He guides whomsoever He will; and He is the All-mighty, the All-wise." In a famous *hadith*, the Prophet was more strongly "predestinarian": "Know that if the nations gather together to benefit you, they will not benefit you unless Allah has decreed it for you. And if the nations gather together to harm you, they will not harm you unless Allah has decreed it for you. The pens have been lifted and the pages have dried."[61] The last sentence (pens lifted and pages dried) is particularly striking, seeming to imply that predecreed actions cannot be altered. However, in another *hadith*, the Prophet negates this premature conclusion; he says: "Good works protect from evil fates. Charity in secret extinguishes the wrath of the Lord, maintaining family ties increases lifespan, and every good deed is charity."[62] In another one, he says: "Nothing repels the divine decree but supplication, and nothing increases lifespan but

---

[61] *Hadith* in Al-Tirmidhi, *Sunan Al-Tirmidhi*, 4:248 #2516, considered authentic (*sahih*).
[62] *Hadith* in Al-Ṭabarani, 1995: 6:163 #6086 – considered authentic (*sahih*).

righteousness."[63] These *hadith*s clearly indicate that divine decrees are not definitive, and humans have some capacity (*qudrah*, or *qadar*) to control and steer their actions. Indeed, in 13:39, the Qur'an states: "Allah effaces what He will, and establishes (what He will), and with Him is the source of ordinance [literally, 'the Mother of the Book']." Humans' free action and responsibility was also famously affirmed by (the caliph) Umar Ibn Al-Khattab, who in the story of a town that had been afflicted by the plague, decided to turn away from it but was questioned (by Abu Ubaydah) "do you run from God's decree?" He replied: "We run from God's decree to God's decree."[64]

From very early times, these ideas produced major theological positions and splits. The Qadriyyah[65] school (early eighth century CE) declared humans' absolute free will and responsibility. The Jabriyyah[66] or Jahmiyyah,[67] then followed by the ("rationalist") Mu'tazila,[68] insisted that God's absolute justice and fairness necessarily implied that humans are responsible for their actions and thus free to choose and act. Finally, the Ash'arite[69] school came up with a "middle way" by introducing the idea of *kasb* (acquisition), whereby God is always the creator of all actions, but humans "acquire" them by their choosing. Muslim scholars from medieval to modern times have taken positions some-where along that spectrum, with Ash'arite theology largely dominating since its emergence in the early 10th century CE.

Modern science introduced two important ideas into these debates: (a) the idea that the same physical processes and outputs necessarily result when the same sets of causes occur, except possibly for quantum processes at submicro-scopic levels; (b) the seminal experiment by Benjamin Libet in 1983 (repeated numerous times since then), which seemed to indicate the existence of hidden mechanisms working in our brains but "covered" by an illusion of free will. If we follow chemical processes from atoms and molecules in our bodies to electrical neurological processes in our brains to thoughts and actions, it seems that each one follows another in a causal chain, hence deterministically. Furthermore, psychologists and psychoanalysts have shown that there are often hidden forces working within us that belie our freedom of behavior, and if Libet's results are correct, actions are worked out in our brains before we become aware of any "decision" we "make."

---

[63] *Hadith* in Al-Tirmidhi, *Sunan Al-Tirmidhi*, 4:16 #2139; considered fair (*hasan*).

[64] The story is related in both Bukhari's (famous) collection of authentic *hadith*s (number 5729) and Muslim's (also famous) collection of authentic *hadith*s (number 2219).

[65] From *qudrah/qadar*, "capacity."

[66] From *jabr*, "compulsion."

[67] After its founder, Jahm Ibn Safwan, second half of the eighth century CE.

[68] From the Arabic root indicating a "withdrawal" (in reference to theological disagreement).

[69] After its founder, Al-Ash'ari, c. 874–936 CE.

Are we programmed biological robots with just enough illusory free will to keep us going and not stop or just kill ourselves? Is free will just an adaptive evolutionary trait that helps people keep doing what is needed for group survival? Or are there "emergent" processes where phenomena occur that are not simply the result of "lower-level" chemical interactions? Can our minds (or even spirits) produce decisions in some "downward causation" process? More and more scientists and philosophers, at least in the West, are convinced that we have no free will. This position tends to go together with materialism/atheism. Muslims object to a total rejection of free will, but if they want to seriously debate the materialists, they will need more than the traditionalist arguments of acquisition under God's absolute creation of all acts.

Randomness

We may define "randomness" simply as the unpredictability of a process or phenomenon. There are two types of randomness. The first one is "fundamental" or "ontological," that is, built into nature: This is what we find in quantum phenomena (assuming these are indeed intrinsically indeterministic, contra Einstein and a minority of scientists who believe that a grander, fully deterministic theory of the microscopic world awaits our formulation). The second one is "epistemic" randomness, where the phenomenon is actually deterministic but too complex and sensitive to initial conditions and parameters to allow for a prediction after some time (this is the case of "chaos").

Randomness of one kind or the other is ubiquitous in nature. The question is how to square this with divine omniscience and benevolence and with the idea of "purpose" in human existence. A number of "random" but momentous events have occurred during the history of life and humanity, including the asteroid that struck Earth some 66 million years ago and triggered the disappearance of the dinosaurs, paving the way for the emergence of primates and humans, randomness in solar activity, and more. Classical/medieval philosophers and theologians, both Muslims (e.g., Ibn Sina, Ibn Rushd) and non-Muslims (e.g., Augustine, Calvin) tended to reject randomness, equating it with haphazardness, which contradicts God's purposeful, omniscient creation and action in the world. Some of those thinkers were more strongly deterministic than others, but they all interpreted "chance" events as simply human ignorance, insisting that God's will is definite and all events are known to him, if mysterious to us.

Recently, a multidisciplinary, multicultural project was conducted on randomness. It resulted in an edited volume titled *Abrahamic Reflections on Randomness and Providence* (Clark and Koperski 2022), including a chapter by Guessoum, "Randomness in the Cosmos." According to Guessoum, first, without quantum randomness, the universe would not have produced galaxies and stars, and then planets and life; the cosmos would have been utterly homogeneous, without structure or complexity. Secondly, all randomness, quantum or chaos-type, satisfies statistical laws; hence individual events are often not predictable, but evolutions of systems are. Thirdly, without randomness, the cosmos, including life and humans, would be completely deterministic, thus ruling out any free will or accountability (Guessoum 2022).

Transsexual Issues

The phenomenon of "intersexuality" has been known since the dawn of humanity. An intersex person is born with mixed or underdeveloped reproductive or sexual organs, thus making it difficult to classify them as male or female, which often requires "rectifying" surgery to be carried out. Classical Islamic jurisprudence has addressed the question of what is to be done in such cases. The general consensus is to surgically "make" the newborn male or female, according to the dominant traits. If the situation is too ambiguous, the parents are advised to wait and see how things develop, including observation of the child's behavior and inclination. If, however, the organs clearly indicate a dominance of male or female characteristics, the person's "inclination" is not to be considered. Modern science has brought new information to help address, or sometimes complicate, the situation. First, the presence of internal organs (e.g., ovaries and fallopian tubes) can easily be checked for, using modern imaging instruments such as ultrasound. More sophisticated genetic tests can examine a newborn's chromosomes to see if they are XY (male) or XX (female). One in 500–1,000 male babies are born with an XXY chromosome set (Klinefelter syndrome); they have normal male genitalia but often develop breasts later.

Modern psychology has further complicated matters, first by distinguishing between "sexual" and "gender" identities. Sex is defined by one's anatomy, which is sometimes complicated. Gender relates to a person's feelings and inclinations. Thus, "gender identity disorders," or "gender dysphoria," sometimes appear. The modern split between "sexual identity" and "gender identity" has led a number of countries to allow people to either change their legal and social status (i.e., change one's name and identify as male, female, or nonbinary, regardless of one's anatomy) or undergo "sexual reassignment" surgery or hormonal treatment. Contemporary Islamic jurisprudence has by and large refused to accept this distinction between sex and gender and rejected the idea that a person can freely and without an anatomically based medical reason decide to change his/her body (by growing or removing breasts, surgically modifying genital organs, etc.). The discussion of transsexual and transgender matters, though much less live than the question of homosexuality, has started to appear in the Arab-Muslim world. Cases of young men or women who have "changed their appearance" (grown or removed breasts, grown beards, etc.) have appeared, with hormonal treatment being available, and surgery being carried out either in semi-secret locations or abroad. Thus, in 2016, the UAE issued a (new) law on transsexuality.

In September 1992, the (influential) Saudi Council of Senior Ulama (Islamic scholars), responding to requests/questions submitted, issued a ruling on trans-sexual transformations, forbidding sex changes when the organs are clearly defined, deeming these attempts to "change God's creation,"[70] and only allow-ing "clarifying" medical procedures (such as surgery or hormone therapy) when the sexual organs are somewhat mixed. In February 1989, the Fiqh Council of the Muslim World League had already issued a ruling with the same stipula-tions. It will be interesting to see how the Western push to distinguish between sexual (anatomical) and gender (psychological and social) identities and the insistence that it is a personal right to identify, choose, and change both one's sexual and gender identities will play out in the Muslim world and how Islamic scholars will react to cases as they increase in that sphere.

Artificial Intelligence

The latest and perhaps most intriguing topic to enter the "science and religion" domain is artificial intelligence (AI).[71] In the Islamic context, discussions and contributions have so far been few and minor, but this is slated to change with the publication of the "Islam and AI" Element in this series. The *Encyclopedia Britannica* defines AI as "the ability of a digital computer or computer-controlled robot to perform tasks commonly associated with intelligent beings … systems endowed with the intellectual processes characteristic of humans, such as the ability to reason, discover meaning, generalize, or learn from past experience."

Recent and significant progress in AI (thanks to faster computers and the availability of "big data") has allowed AI to help humans solve complex problems and produce valuable applications, including (so far): face and object recognition, text and speech analysis and translation, more accurate medical diagnoses, online

---

[70] Referring to the Qur'anic verse (3:119), "[']And I will lead them astray, and fill them with fancies and I will command them and they will cut off the cattle's ears; I will command them and they will alter God's creation.' Whoso takes Satan to him for a friend, instead of God, has surely suffered a manifest loss," and the *hadith* "May God curse the tattooed, men and women, and women who pluck their eyebrows or make gaps between their front teeth (to display beauty), changing the creation of God Almighty" (narrated by Abdallah Ibn Masood and reported by Bukhari and Muslim).

[71] See, among others: Singler 2017; Cheong 2020; Reed 2021.

user profiling and personalized recommendations, self-driving vehicles, and so on. Most spectacularly, AI has defeated the best chess and go players, produced proofs of mathematical theorems, and generated works of art, to name its achievements in just a few "high-intelligence" domains. No wonder people are anticipating the construction of a machine with general artificial intelligence that can surpass humans in all areas; such a machine may become independent, possibly conscious, and perhaps dangerous.

Even before we get there, AI is already affecting our behavior, our perceptions of humanity and its values, and our beliefs. Is a superintelligent, conscious, omniscient (networked, with access to all available knowledge) and omnipotent (connected, and therefore able to command anything anywhere) machine not a god? Can we build unchangeable rules into such a machine to ensure that it will always serve virtuous higher principles and human values? Which principles and values should be imposed on all AI/robot machines? Some such values may be universally accepted, for example, justice/fairness, honesty/truth, tolerance/respect, forgiveness, and so on; but others, including those that are explicitly religious, may be contentious, for example, spiritual growth, higher (afterlife) purposes, obedience to God's rules, and more. Even more distressing is the (real) possibility of AI technology soon combining with genetic engineering (to create "enhanced" organs or humans), nanotechnology (tiny robots performing various tasks, some of them inside human bodies), and the creation of brain–machine networks, and the like, developments which are often referred to as "transhumanism."

AI thus needs to be interpreted against the backdrop of the religious/Islamic worldview (and its position on God, nature, and the place of humans in the universe) and the general purposes and ethics of human life, that is, a harmonious relationship with other humans (individuals and groups), with other creatures, with nature as a whole, and with God. A recent paper (Raquib et al. 2022) advances a holistic Islamic virtue-based AI ethics framework grounded in the context of Islamic objectives (*maqasid*) as an alternative ethical system for AI governance. We hope to see many more works (coming from Muslim and other perspectives) engaging with this vital topic.

Transhumanism

The *Encyclopedia Britannica* defines[72] "transhumanism" as a "social and philosophical movement devoted to promoting the research and development of robust human-enhancement technologies ... Such modifications resulting from the addition of biological or physical technologies would be more or less permanent

---

[72] René Ostberg, "Transhumanism," *Britannica*, n.d., www.britannica.com/topic/transhumanism.

and integrated into the human body." Biohackers have already modified their bodies by inserting chips that can control or be controlled at a distance, and Elon Musk's Neuralink company is conducting projects to insert chips in animals' brains, allowing researchers to read those brains and command them remotely. Such radical and permanent modifications to the human body and mind raise a host of ethical issues: Is it good or bad to drastically increase humans' capabilities in vision, other senses and muscles, in cognitive capabilities, in life expectancy, and so on, to a super-human level? Is that "playing God"? Will it split humanity into a large "1.0" majority and a small, rich "2.0" minority? How much can humans be modified and still be human? What is "being human"? To what extent are we defined by our bodies and our capabilities? What does it mean if we extend our lifespan to hundreds or possibly thousands of years? Should we hold on to our weaknesses as defining features of our humanness, or shall we strive for "perfection" (at least asymptotically)?

Muslim thinkers and researchers have started to engage with this topic (Mavani 2014; Bouzenita 2018; Hejazi 2019). They emphasize that corrective procedures and prosthetics are certainly permissible and even encouraged to rectify any defect or accident, assuming that these do not lead to drastic changes in the nature (shape and capability) of the patient. Humanity is even encouraged to seek betterments in its livelihood (more comfort, longer lives, etc.[73]), so long as these goals are in line with the divine purposes of creation and existence. However, the Qur'an contains stern warnings against drastic modifications of humans, animals, and the rest of creation. Indeed, Muslim scholars often remind everyone of the Qur'an's origin story of Adam when he was tempted by "the devil," who promised him immortality (Q 7:20) and power that "does not wane" (20:120). Indeed, "the devil" told God of his plan to "mislead them (humans) and create in them false desires ... and command them to change Allah's creation " (4:119).

Conclusion

In addition to their complexity, fluidity, and urgency, what makes ongoing discussions particularly intriguing and testing is their *global character*. Scientific discoveries and innovations are almost instantly shared and debated by the community of experts the world over, followed by other intellectuals and the larger public. Technological transformation has rapid worldwide repercussions, and it impacts users who, in order to cope with change and in the attempt to respond to unprecedented questions (including dramatic moral dilemmas), may turn to traditional narratives, texts, and authorities for answers or

---

[73] Hamid Mavani even says "extending healthy human life *indefinitely* could be accommodated within the Islamic religious system" (Mavani 2014: 78, emphasis added).

directives. While taking up new challenges, Islam is therefore confronted with, and participates in, a global, intercultural, and interreligious conversation. Or, to put it somewhat more pessimistically, if Muslim thinkers were *not* to take up such challenges, they would condemn themselves and Islam to irrelevance in many vital sectors and developments of contemporary society.

5 'Islam and Science' in Education and the Wider Culture

'Islam and Science' in Education

Education is a crucial area in which Islam and science interact, in urgent need of research and action. The dynamics of education involve multiple actors, levels, and factors, all intertwined in complex ways that warrant careful unpacking. Official educational policies impose orientations and constraints on curricula and pedagogy, based on various factors and objectives. Science instructors carry worldviews into the classroom, including particular perceptions of religion, science, and their relation. Students then respond to the (loaded) teaching based on their own prior knowledge and understanding of science, religion, society, and culture, including influences of public campaigns and debates, both local and global. The topic that perhaps provides the best glimpse of such complex interactions is the teaching of biological evolution.

Elise K. Burton (2010) has meticulously scrutinized science curricula that are implemented in several Middle Eastern countries (Iran, Saudi Arabia, Turkey, and Israel). Burton's research combines a comparative analysis of official documents and textbooks with a sociological and historical approach. Comparing the curricula in Saudi Arabia and Iran is instructive. In both countries, religion is a driving force, and education is strongly centralized (curricula and textbooks are developed for all schools by the respective ministries of education), but marked differences can be found in the teaching of evolution. An official 2006 Saudi policy document states that science education is aimed at showing the Islamic contribution to science, as well as the "perfect harmony between science and religion in Islam." Saudi textbooks are often interspersed with Qur'anic verses that make reference to natural phenomena. An official 2009 Iranian science education document is much subtler in its references to God and presents science as a field separate from religion; it also stresses goals such as fostering critical thinking and promoting scientific literacy among the citizenry. A major difference between the Saudi and the Iranian educational system emerges regarding the theory of evolution. The approach promoted by Saudi textbooks is simply creationist. A tenth-grade textbook mentions "adaptation," though not in the context of the theory of evolution, but as evidence of divine creation. A twelfth-grade textbook explicitly states that humans were directly created by God, depicting Darwin as the proponent of a "Western" theory that lacked proof and was supported through unwarranted speculations and frauds; according to the textbook, it is a theory that has been embraced by some Muslims, whose stance therefore qualifies as "blasphemy." Iranian students are introduced to the theory of evolution as early as in the fifth grade. While formulated in simple terms, evolution of nonhuman life forms is presented as supported by empirical evidence, and it is stressed that the authorities in charge of examining and validating such evidence are geologists and scientists. Subsequently, eighth-grade textbooks provide an explanation of evolution with adaptations being related to changes and selection. Finally, a high-school textbook with a forty-page chapter on evolution presents Darwin's ideas, including a biographical profile and the statement that his theory is accepted by "nearly all biologists." However, Iranian textbooks are almost silent on human evolution.

Pierre Clément (2015) studied the perception of evolution by teachers in 28 countries, with a total of 2,130 Muslim teachers in 12 of those countries. He found a strong resistance to evolution in countries where nearly all teachers are Muslim (Algeria, Morocco, Tunisia, and Senegal). Nevertheless, in countries where only some teachers are Muslim (e.g., Lebanon, Burkina Faso), there was no difference, or sometimes very little, between Muslim and Christian teachers. The country's history and social dynamics, including religious practices, were found to have more important effects. Indeed, the more teachers believed in God and practiced their religion, the more creationist they were likely to be, regardless of their respective religion. Some religious teachers, however, accepted evolution, considering it as being governed by God. Nasser Mansour (2019), an Egyptian science education specialist, has conducted research about the views of Egyptian science teachers on science and religion issues and how such views inform their pedagogy. According to some teachers, religion and science are in *conflict*; that is, science clashes with religion, as the two provide widely different teachings on topics such as the origin and evolution of humanity, planet Earth, the universe, and so on. Some teachers view science and religion as *independent*. Others seem view them in *dialogue,* although what they mean is in fact that religion should provide those answers that science is not able to attain, or that religion should provide ethical guidance. A large number of teachers view science and religion as *integrated*, that is, either complementing each other or seeing science as being contained in Islam or even in the Qur'an.[74]

---

[74] Mansour adopted Barbour's (2000) taxonomy of possible science–religion relations: conflict, independence, dialogue, or integration.

Another factor affecting the teaching of evolution is public campaigns that are conducted against the theory in certain places. In Turkey, evolution was included in the biology curriculum after the foundation of the Republic (1923). However, after the 1980 military coup, creationism was sneaked into biology textbooks and Darwin's ideas were criticized, while students had to take mandatory religious courses. Evolution was presented as a marginal "view" rather than a central and unifying theory, and only students who chose a science track in high school were learning it. Additionally, scientists defending evolution were the target of public campaigns, and the creation–evolution debate was extensively covered by national media (see Peker et al. 2010; Muğaloğlu 2018). Finally, in 2017, the Turkish government produced a new precollege curriculum with sweeping changes, where the only chapter on evolution, "The Beginning of Life and Evolution," was removed from high-school textbooks, and all references to Darwinian theory were deleted. It was argued that "students don't have the necessary scientific background and information-based context needed to comprehend" the evolution debates (Genç 2018; Karapehlivan 2019).

A discussion of the treatment of science in Islamic educational contexts must cover the Gülen movement's school network and its curriculum. A good resource for this topic is Caroline Tee's book (2016), in particular its chapters on science and education. The movement is led by Turkish author and preacher Muhammed Fethullah Gülen (b. 1941), and its theology is based on that of Said Nursi (see section 2 of this Element). The movement's educational institutions (from nurseries to universities) number around 500, according to Tee. The general curriculum emphasizes the importance of combining science and faith, with a rather conservative slant; its institutions observe gender segregation, for instance. It is, however, characterized by excellence in the natural sciences, with outstanding performance in the Science Olympics and students regularly securing places at top universities. In Tee's assessment, this pursuit of excellence in scientific subjects is simply pragmatic; indeed, she finds no evidence for any promotion of scientific research. In fact, Gülenist pedagogy and its curriculum do not promote critical and creative thought, but rather a rote-learning style of education.

On issues related to science and Islam, we must note that Gülen's literature presents evolution as "Darwinism" (an ideology), a vessel of materialism and atheism, and sees it as an unproven "theory," incompatible with human dignity. Differently from Harun Yahya (Adnan Oktar), the Gülen movement does not promote and disseminate its creationist material internationally. However, despite the rejection of, and frequent derision toward evolution expressed among its community members, the relevant scientific material is covered in classes, especially in higher grades, without reference to Islamic ideas. Students are expected to master evolutionary concepts in the interest of winning competitions and as a preparation for higher education.

Making a larger point about how Islam and science should relate properly in education, Nasser Mansour writes: "In cultures where religion has a major influence on people's lives, the development of science curricula should be made in a partnership between science educators and religion scholars, especially with regard to socio-scientific issues associated with religion" (Mansour 2019: 332). This, he explains, would result in a dynamic enterprise, subject to frequent updating and considering scientific and technological advancements; ideally, in collaboration with actual scientists.

Other scholars have proposed various strategies that could allow for a proper and constructive interaction between Islam and science in education. Rana Dajani, molecular biologist at the Hashemite University (Jordan), is convinced that evolution, including human origins, should be taught to Muslim students not only as a key element of scientific knowledge, but also as a way to foster critical thinking. She argues that Islamic creationism and Muslim reluctance to accept evolution are byproducts of colonialism; that is, they resulted from the hasty adoption of Western/Christian views hostile to evolution. Dajani recalls how some students complained to her administrators that she was "preaching against Islam" after she had explained evolution; in response, she pointed out that her teaching adhered to the books that the university had officially adopted. Dajani offers her students detailed evidence for evolution, as well as a methodology with which to deal with apparent discrepancies between scientific findings and Qur'anic passages. However, whether a student accepts evolution or not is not crucial in how she marks their papers: "I do not want my students to write that they accept evolution just to pass an exam" (Dajani 2015).

Jamal Mimouni, professor of physics at the University of Constantine (Algeria), offers critical (and indeed slightly pessimistic) reflections on the presence of religion in the science classroom (Mimouni 2015). He observes that in the Arab-Muslim world, interest in and a stated respect for the natural sciences are not always paired with an actual understanding of the scientific method. Hence, he does not see how Islam could safely and properly be brought into science classrooms. He dismisses S. H. Nasr's vision of merging spirituality with science, based on the various objections that have been expressed against his *scientia sacra*. He also considers the proposed "Rushdian" methodology (i.e., inspired by Ibn Rushd's harmonizing ideas), according to which the scriptures should be reinterpreted in the light of established knowledge/science any time there seems to be a conflict between the former and the latter, but he maintains that this approach could only be a tool for academic debates or possibly for informal discussions with students. Other options he considers include courses in the history of science with an emphasis on Muslim figures and their approaches; courses in ecology with an emphasis on Islamic values; and multidisciplinary "bridging" courses with an emphasis on scientific literacy, aligned with Islamic values. However, Mimouni points out that such courses would need doubly competent teachers and that students might perceive them as being useless for their goal of gaining specialized knowledge.

Nidhal Guessoum, who teaches at the American University of Sharjah (UAE), shares Mimouni's concern for the state of scientific education in the Muslim world, pointing out its failures in terms of teaching the distinction between scientific and religious knowledge. He observes, however, that simply telling students that their views are wrong (e.g., on evolution) or that the Qur'an should be left out of a scientific discussion is not a constructive and fruitful option. If dismissed, students will feel antagonized, their wrong views will not have been corrected, and their reference to the Qur'an will not have been addressed. Guessoum is therefore in favor of the creation of "bridging" courses, either taught by instructors with double competency or by interdisciplinary teams. In such courses, religion and science may interact according to a SOMA model, or "softly overlapping magisteria"; in other words, issues at the interface of science and religion would be carefully unpacked while firmly adhering to some key principles and ideas, including the scientific method (particularly the concepts of "theory," "facts," "laws," etc.) and the neutrality of science vis-à-vis worldviews and religion, all while stressing the fact that the adoption of a naturalistic methodology does not imply the nonexistence of God. Guessoum warns that such courses may carry some risks: in particular, the possible "sneaking in" of creationism and pseudoscience (especially in the form of *i'jaz*) (Guessoum 2018).

One interdisciplinary course on Islam and science is offered by Stefano Bigliardi at Al Akhawayn University in Ifrane, an English-speaking liberal arts university in Morocco. Such courses (taught under the title of "History of Ideas") have been offered almost uninterruptedly each semester since fall 2016, including a number of summer sessions. A recent syllabus of this course[75] lists three overarching intended learning outcomes: (1) to get a historical overview of the science–religion debate, with a focus on nineteenth-, twentieth-, and twenty-first-century discussions in the Muslim world, going back to the Galileo affair, covering Darwin's theory of evolution, and reaching up to Bucaille, Sardar, Harun Yahya, Guessoum, and others; (2) to adopt and engage with Ian G. Barbour's typology for the interaction of religion and science (Barbour

---

[75] "Fall 2021 – SHSS – AUI – History of Ideas – 'Islam and the Quest for Modern Science,'" (2021), www.academia.edu/72204008/Fall_2021_SHSS_AUI_History_of_Ideas_Islam_and_the_Quest_for_Modern_Science.

2000); and (3) to formulate a well-argued opinion on the theories, ideas, and controversies covered based on using the technical and philosophical vocabulary needed to discuss science and religion, including concepts like "scientific theory," "supernatural miracle," and so on. The course echoes Philip Clayton's and Mark S. Railey's recommendation that a science and religion course should be "an advocacy for the discipline of science and religion itself rather than for any one particular theological agenda within the discipline" (Clayton and Railey 1998: 129).

To be sure, while designing such courses, anticipating and mitigating challenges is crucial. Careful attention must be paid to political, cultural, institutional, and even individual aspects, in order to avoid counterproductive friction at various levels as well as pedagogic ineffectiveness. That being said, some perceived challenges may in fact be opportunities in disguise, and students may be more receptive, collaborative, and varied than anticipated. The fact that students come to class with strong beliefs makes for increased opportunities to engage in cooperative learning and lively debates. Additionally, while it is safe to assume that *most* students will be familiar with (and supportive of) views hostile to evolution and/or appreciative of *i'jaz*, one can also expect that a few students will self-identify as atheist and will be familiar with discussions of evolution *à la* Richard Dawkins, while some others will entertain more "liberal" views on religion as harmonizable with evolution. All such students, if provided with an adequate "safe space" and a serene learning atmosphere, will be eager to express and debate their views, often enriching their initial viewpoint or even changing it. Finally, courses on Islam and science offer opportunities to explore and appreciate local or regional figures that would otherwise be left untapped or insufficiently capitalized on by typical education in high school and at university. For instance, students may have heard of, but never examined and discussed, the ideas of a major philosopher like Ibn Rushd, or important paleontological discoveries made in their country (e.g., the remains of *Homo sapiens* discovered in Morocco), or the achievements and views of contemporary Muslim scientists. However, a major problem that warrants careful discussion is whether the "intended learning outcomes" of a course should be considered fully achieved if a student persists in their belief in creationism, in *i'jaz*, or in various forms of pseudoscience.

'Islam and Science' in the General Culture

It is difficult to rigorously assess the general public's views on Islam and Science (and how they should be related) because of the simple fact that there are essentially no surveys or studies of this topic covering the Muslim world.

In fact, there is almost no data on scientific literacy or the more qualitative "culture of science" in today's Muslim societies (in contrast to the existence of rich data[76] from many other countries). What we are left with is our (somewhat subjective) observations and personal experience of how people perceive the relationship between Islam and modern science. Indeed, we have numerous cases and manifestations, which – though anecdotal – in the aggregate produce a rather somber picture. In particular, the popularity of *i'jaz* has not waned, despite the increase in critiques expressed by Muslim authors in the last decade or so.

In the foreword to this Element, we (briefly) related the striking story of a Tunisian doctoral student who, in 2017, submitted a thesis in which she combined deep misunderstandings of science with literal and superficial readings of the Qur'an and the *hadith*, trying to prove that the Earth is flat and rests in the center of the universe. Two years earlier, another incident took place in the UAE and caused reverberations around the world. In February 2015, a three-minute video appeared on YouTube, showing a Saudi sheikh declaring that the Earth does not move, whether around itself or around the Sun, also presenting "evidence" for this claim, some of it religious and some scientific (according to him). Sheikh Bandar Al-Khaibari affirmed to his audience, which included university students, that first Allah created the "heavenly house" (*al bayt al-ma'mur*) directly above the Kaaba, and if the Earth rotated or revolved (around anything), the "heavenly house" would be forced to move (and this could not be). Second, if the Earth rotated west to east, a plane would never reach China; or, if the Earth rotated east to west, a plane should just take off vertically and wait for China to come below. He further dismissed other claims made by scientists, adding a touch of "conspiracism," by saying, "They say they went to the moon, but these are just Hollywood stories. "

Some Arab-Muslim commentators tried to downplay his statements by citing polls showing that even today in the United States, 25 percent of the population think that the Sun revolves around the Earth, not the other way around. However, this ignorance in the West is not based on "religious knowledge" and is not championed and presented by a religious figure or to an educated public. In fact, those familiar with contemporary Islamic writings know that Al-Khaibari's claims, although rare among current Muslim *'ulama* (religious scholars), have been carried and sometimes expressed by a number of

---

[76] See the US National Science Foundation survey 'Science and Technology: Public Attitudes, Knowledge, and Interest' (https://ncses.nsf.gov/pubs/nsb20207/), conducted every three years in a dozen countries and the 2014 report on science culture "Science Culture: Where Canada Stands," Council of Canadian Academies, August 28, 2014 (https://cca-reports.ca/reports/science-culture-where-canada-stands/) conducted in a dozen countries.

prominent Saudi clerics of recent years (the late Sheikh Bin Baz, Sheikh Al-Tuwaijri, Sheikh Al-Fawzan, and others) who defend the concept of a stationary Earth and do their best to dissuade the learning of modern astronomy in their country. *Fatwa*s have even been issued on this subject, but everyone has more or less ignored them, and the rotation of the Earth and its revolution around the Sun continue to be taught to students in the Arab-Muslim world, including in Saudi Arabia. However, for several years now we have witnessed a daring and sustained social-media campaign rejecting the "Western theories" that the Earth revolves around the Sun, that Americans have walked on the moon, and the rest of NASA's "claims" (NASA now has a bad reputation in some Arab social circles).

Serious discussions have taken place following the above "incidents," raising the following questions: Are these cases just rare anomalies to be ignored or do they represent the visible part of an iceberg? Does the fact that the arguments presented against modern knowledge, whether by the sheikh or the doctoral student, were essentially religious (based on *hadith*s or verses taken literally) indicate that Muslims generally have great difficulty in harmonizing modern science with their religious beliefs? Why do we have students at the highest academic levels and religious scholars who still have not digested basic knowledge of the world and the relationship between this knowledge and religious beliefs? What should be done to prevent students from finding themselves in this bewildering situation at the end of their education?

Some insights can be gleaned by looking more closely at the Tunisian student's doctoral thesis.[77] Its general conclusions show a literalist approach to the Qur'an and the *hadith* as well as a very poor understanding of the scientific methods which allow us to declare certain knowledge as facts and not scientific "opinions" or "models." Moreover, the doctoral student, presenting her "plate-geocentric model," mixed – sometimes in the same sentence – religious "arguments" and scientific data. In fact, in her conclusion we find a statement according to which she is proposing "A new vision of the kinematics of objects in accordance with the verses of the Qur'an"; or "The geocentric model is thus repaired by the modification of the sphericity of the earth by the flattening and the modification of the orbits of the celestial bodies while in accordance with the verses of the Qur'an and the declarations of our Prophet"

---

[77] The thesis itself was never published or made public; we only know its conclusions from what Hafedh Ateb, former president of the Tunisian Astronomical Society, published on his Facebook page on April 1, 2017: www.facebook.com/hafedh.ateb/posts/10211022808878459. The student and her PhD supervisor had, a few months earlier, published a "paper" titled "The Geocentric Model of the Earth: Physics and Astronomy Arguments" in the predatory journal *The International Journal of Science & Technoledge* (www.theijst.com); the paper was removed from the website when the scandal broke, but only after we had downloaded a copy.

(our translation). More widely, flat-earthism has lately made a comeback, spreading like wildfire through social media in particular. Googling "flat earth" in Arabic, we get 138,000 hits and 51,000 videos, and specifically 61,700 references for "flat earth in the Qur'an." While some of these webpages and videos may be refutations of flat-earthism, the explosion of this topic and debates around it is cause for concern.

The rejection of established knowledge is not limited to the "flat earth" topic. Astrology, too, is having a renaissance: A number of websites have reported that traffic to their horoscope pages has, in the last few years, increased exponentially – in one case by 150 percent in one year.

An interesting project pertaining to general-public activity in the field of Islam and science is the video portal constructed by Salman Hameed, director of the Center for the Study of Science in Muslim Societies at Hampshire College (USA) and his team between 2014 and 2017.[78] The project evaluated some 220 videos from the internet (YouTube, Vimeo, Dailymotion, etc.) whose creators combined ideas from Islam and from science, sometimes adding elements of history. Hameed's team then provided a short summary and assessment of each video, along with symbols to denote positive (accurate, widely accepted), negative (erroneous or odd ideas), or null content on the subjects of Islam, science, and history (each separately).

'Islam and Science' and Current Events (Coronavirus, Climate Change, Etc.)

The coronavirus pandemic affected world religions in various and unprecedented ways, raising a number of questions. Was this an act of God, some test or punishment? Should the faithful rely on medicine and science or pray and trust in their faiths? Will God intervene and rid humanity of the pandemic if many devout people offer heartfelt prayers? More generally, the pandemic reignited the debate between religion and reason/science. In the Islamic context, the same trends that are usually witnessed in the Islam and science debates reemerged: *i'jaz* claims, rationalizations, fideist approaches, and so on. For example, on the more scientific or rational side, many chose to focus on the Prophet's recommendations on hygiene, generally, and behavior during epidemics, in particular, citing *hadith*s that instructed Muslims to "shelter in place" when an outbreak occurred in one's town, and more generally to seek medical treatment for any

---

[78] https://sites.hampshire.edu/scienceandislamvideoportal/ Hameed, an astronomer by training, also campaigns for the understanding of science in the Urdu-speaking world with media programs in which he popularizes astronomy and cosmology for Muslim viewers.

illness. Many declared the Prophet as prescient, even reading "social distancing" in some of his statements.

Another major issue facing humanity more and more urgently, and on which religious leaders have had to speak and take action, is climate change. In August 2015, forty or so Islamic scholars, policymakers, and Muslim social activists gathered in Istanbul to discuss climate change and other environmental and planet-related issues. They issued a bold, well-informed, and wide-ranging declaration[79] that set clear targets on greenhouse emissions (phase out by 2050) and energy sources (complete replacement by renewable sources by 2050). The declaration reminded Muslims of their religious responsibilities and duties to safeguard the planet, asking: "What will future generations say of us, who leave them a degraded planet as our legacy? How will we face our Lord and Creator?" It also pointed to a host of environmental, ecological, and socioeconomic issues that require immediate and serious attention: global and local climate changes; contamination and befoulment of atmosphere, lands, water systems, and seas; soil erosion, deforestation and desertification; damage to human health, including a host of modern-day diseases, and others. Furthermore, it presented a list of Islamic moral and behavioral principles to live by for the betterment of our planet and human communities.

Concluding Remarks

The general public suffers from multiple confusions on a number of issues: what science really says and how it works, what looks like science but actually is not (pseudoscience), and how science and religion/Islam should relate. One of the main causes for this general confusion, and one which keeps growing, is social media. The new tools of connection and exchange between people have leveled the playing field: It does not matter how much or how little education or expertise one has on a given topic, one's impact is proportional to the number of "friends"/followers one has. And should a scientist dare to brandish their expertise on a topic, they are immediately attacked as "elitist." Furthermore, social media makes it easier for people to cling to their long-held (often erroneous) views by circulating supportive evidence for those ideas (what is known as "confirmation bias"). Indeed, changing minds is often an uphill battle.

What can we do? First, science educators need to be fully aware of these trends and of their causes. Secondly, our educational curricula and methods need to take the above biases and social conditions into account. In particular, before teaching any scientific knowledge, educators must address their

---

[79] *Islamic Declaration on Global Climate Change*, IFEES/EcoIslam, n.d., www.ifees.org.uk/wp-content/uploads/2020/01/climate_declarationmmwb.pdf

audience's deeply held ideas (often a result of their religious backgrounds and education) and make students aware that "obvious facts" are often wrong. Accurate knowledge and understanding can be acquired in a coherent and long-lasting manner only after misconceptions and fallacies in reasoning have been exposed and corrected. Educators, writers, broadcasters, and opinion makers have an important role to play in correcting the damage that digital media and platforms are inflicting on the young generation, often by spreading pseudo-science and sometimes basing it on religion.

6 General Conclusions: Lessons and Prospects

While offering this brief, somewhat detailed, and sometimes opinionated recon-struction of mostly modern and contemporary discussions of Islam and the sciences to our readers, we have often touched upon the multiple and inter-twined *challenges* that such explorations represent. For instance, we have highlighted the methodological weaknesses undermining some of the sophisti-cated discussions of Islam and science that have taken place, such as Al-Faruqi's idea of Islamizing knowledge/science or Nasr's proposal to revive old versions of science infused with mysticism and supernaturalism – two projects advanced by remarkable thinkers, presenting intellectual merits while carrying some heavy baggage that readers need to be made aware of. We have also drawn attention to the strong subscription, among the general public but also among many educated people, to *i'jaz*, a bold claim as to the miraculous existence of (presumed) accurate, modern scientific content in the Qur'an and the Sunnah that often borders on, or even overlaps with, pseudoscience and carries various kinds of scientific and intellectual flaws. Furthermore, we have hinted at the risk of oversimplifying the interaction between Islam/religion and science, especially in regard to metaphysical and ethical issues, a risk that one may find in the recommendation, made by prominent figures like Abdus Salam, Hoodbhoy, and others, that the two spheres just be kept totally separate, or even that religion should be ignored or rejected altogether (Edis). We have observed and deplored the uncompromising attitude, again in both the general public and some educated circles, toward certain topics that are often perceived as being too sensitive to allow for any discussion or warranting any nuanced interpret-ation. Indeed, it is not uncommon to hear that narratives not presenting "mir-acles" as supernatural events are un-Islamic or that biological evolution cannot possibly be compatible with Islamic faith.

We have indicated that discussions of several new, hot topics, including technology-related ethical dilemmas that call for an evaluation in the light of Islamic principles, have so far remained underdeveloped or even nearly

unexplored in contrast with such debates within other religious traditions. We
have briefly reviewed some studies that clearly suggest the inadequacy of the
educational framework of 'Islam and science' topics, particularly evolution,
across the Muslim world. Indeed, we have tried to look at how the interaction or
interface of Islam with modern science plays out in the "real" world, beyond
academic discussions. Thus, in addition to the educational arena, we have
considered the general public's perception of issues of Islam and science, the
role of social media, and the spread of pseudoscience in connection to Islam
(and religion more generally). We have thus insisted on the importance of
designing effective pedagogical approaches and tools for science teaching and
science communication in the cultural context of the Muslim world. Needless to
say, there are significant challenges in this field, including the navigation of
governmental educational policies and media as well as "local" attitudes that are
shaped by debates and campaigns which are often superficial, acrimonious, and
antagonistic.

Wrapping up the results of our exploration, however, we would like to
equally emphasize the multiple great *opportunities* that discussions at the
interface of Islam and science also represent. Indeed, we think that while the
development of such debates and research calls for intense commitment and
requires a great deal of work, it also presents several hopeful and exciting
prospects that largely exceed the drawbacks. On the whole, the history of the
debates so far shows that even when their responses had significant weaknesses,
many Muslim scholars have taken up the challenge of reconciling Islam and
modern science, displaying remarkable and encouraging thoughtfulness and
insight and critical thinking, as well as paying attention to interfaith concerns
and intercultural dialogues. Additionally, the need to examine both science
itself and its relation to religion and philosophy has led to efforts to review
medieval and ancient contributions by Muslim and other scholars, reviving an
interest in the history of science and philosophy in Islamic civilization in
particular, with serious examinations of various classical works.

We feel that all such intellectual enterprises, if pursued with commitment and
rigor, are bound to bring about not only the flourishing of specific fields and an
overall novel and deeper appreciation of the Islamic heritage, but also a fruitful
dialogue between specialists of different disciplines, including the humanities
and the natural sciences. Moreover, an engagement with science education and
science literacy, both presenting interesting challenges, can provide an impetus
for larger-scale reflections (and exemplary paradigm shifts) in regard to *general*
education and literacy. We want to particularly stress the important opportunities that the field presents today more than ever. While a number of topics may
still appear controversial and thus their investigation and debate is inhibited

(e.g., human evolution, miracles, divine action, transsexual issues, transhumanism, etc.), we believe they represent fertile terrain for young scholars to plow, which could prove fruitful for thought-provoking explorations in academic settings and in public fora.

Last but not least, the engagement of Islam and the sciences provides a valuable platform for intercultural and interreligious debate, beyond traditional borders and perceived divisions. For instance, religious and nonreligious scholars and educators, while disagreeing on various core issues, may still find common cause in rejecting and combating pseudoscience, antiscience, and scientific malpractice, and unite in the support of scientific literacy and the promotion of scientific thinking. We are also convinced that the *variety* of responses – including sometimes strongly diverging ones – that experts can offer on specific questions is an indication and a source of intellectual vitality and richness. In all these regards, the debates on Islam and science can play a globally exemplary role. It is our hope and ambition that the Elements series in Islam and the sciences will not only provide a map and showcase for the value and complexity of the debates in this field, but also function as a platform for their advancement and enrichment.

References

Abduh, M. (1972). *Al-A'mal al-kamila* [Complete Works], vol. 2, ed. M. Umara. Beirut: Dar Al-Shuruq.

Ahmad, A. M. L. (2006). *Al-Talqih al-sina'i bayna aqwal al-atibba' wa-ara' al-fuqaha'* [Artificial Insemination, Physicians' and Jurists' Views]. Alexandria: Dar Al-Fikr Al-Jama'i, 242.

Al-Akiti, M. A. (2016). Reinterpreting Al Ghazali's Alleged Opposition to Science. In U. Hasan & A. Osama (eds.), *Islam and Science: Muslim Responses to Science's Big Questions*. www.academia.edu/39876520/Islam_and_Science_Muslim_Responses_to_Sciences_Big_Questions.

Al-Attas, S. M. N. (1989). *Islam and the Philosophy of Science*. Kuala Lumpur: ISTAC.

Al-Azmeh, A. (1996). *Islams and Modernities*. 2nd ed. London: Verso.

Al-Faruqi, I. R. (1995). *Al Tawhid: Its Implications for Thought and Life*. 3rd ed. Herndon, VA: International Institute of Islamic Thought.

Al-Jisr, H. (1887). *Al-Risala al-Hamidiyya fi haqiqat al-diyana al-Islamiyya wa-haqiqat l-Shari'a al-Muhammadiyya* [A Hamidian Essay on the Truthfulness of the Islamic Religion and the Truthfulness of the Islamic Canon Law]. Beirut: Majlis Ma'arif Wilayat Bayrut.

Al-Khalifi, A. (1998). *Al-Fi'l al-Ilahi bayna al-wujub wa-l-ikhtiyar* [Divine Action between Necessity and Choice]. In *Proceedings of the Third International Conference on Islamic Philosophy*. Cairo: Cairo University Press.

Anawati, G. C. (1979). Philosophy, Theology, and Mysticism. In J. Schacht & C. E. Bosworth (eds.), *The Legacy of Islam*. 2nd ed. Oxford: Clarendon Press, 350–391.

Aramesh, K., & Shadi, H. (2007). Euthanasia: An Islamic Ethical Perspective. *Iranian Journal of Allergy, Asthma and Immunology*, 6(Suppl. 5), 35–38.

Averroes [Ibn Rushd]. (2008). *Tahafut al-Tahafut* [*The Incoherence* of the *Incoherence*], trans. S. van den Bergh, reprint. London: Luzac & Co.

Averroes. [Ibn Rushd]. (2017). *The Decisive Treatise: The Connection between Islamic Religious Law and Philosophy*, ed. M. Campanini. Piscataway, NJ: Gorgias Press.

Azadegan, E. (2014). Islamic Science: A Missed Subject in Bigliardi's Monograph? *Social Epistemology Review and Reply Collective*, 3(10), 12–15. https://social-epistemology.com/2014/09/08/islamic-science-a-missed-subject-in-bigliardis-monograph-ebrahim-azadegan/.

Barbour, I. G. (2000). *When Science Meets Religion: Enemies, Strangers, or Partners?* San Francisco, CA: HarperSanFrancisco.

Bigliardi, S. (2011). Snakes from Staves? Science, Scriptures and the Supernatural in Maurice Bucaille. *Zygon, 46*(4), 793–805.

Bigliardi, S. (2012). The Strange Case of Dr. Bucaille: Notes for a Re-examination. *The Muslim World, 102*(2), 248–263.

Bigliardi, S. (2013). The Interpretation of Miracles According to Mutahhari and Golshani: Comparative and Critical Notes. *Journal of Shi'a Islamic Studies, 6*(3), 261–288.

Bigliardi, S. (2014a). The Contemporary Debate on the Harmony between Islam and Science: Emergence and Challenges of a New Generation. *Social Epistemology, 28*(2), 167–186.

Bigliardi, S. (2014b). *Islam and the Quest for Modern Science: Conversations with Adnan Oktar, Mehdi Golshani, M. Basil Altaie, Zaghloul El-Naggar, Bruno Guiderdoni, and Nidhal Guessoum.* Istanbul: Swedish Research Institute in Istanbul.

Bigliardi, S. (2014c). On Harmonizing Islam and Science: A Response to Edis and a Self-Criticism. *Social Epistemology Review and Reply Collective, 3*(6), 56–68. https://social-epistemology.com/2014/05/15/on-harmonizing-islam-and-science-a-response-to-edis-and-a-self-criticism-stefano-bigliardi/.

Bigliardi, S. (2014d). Mehdi Golshani's Philosophy, Islamic Science(s), and Judeo-Christian/Muslim Dialogue: A Reply to Azadegan. *Social Epistemology Review and Reply Collective, 3*(10), 167–186. https://social-epistemology.com/2014/09/10/mehdi-golshanis-philosophy-islamic-sciences-and-judeo-christianmuslim-dialogue-a-reply-to-azadegan-stefano-bigliardi/.

Bigliardi, S. (2014e). What We Talk about When We Talk about *i'jaz. Social Epistemology Review and Reply Collective, 4*(1), 38–45. https://social-epistemology.com/2014/12/15/what-we-talk-about-when-we-talk-about-i%CA%BFjaz-stefano-bigliardi/.

Bigliardi, S. (2016). Exploring the Contemporary Debate over Islam and Science in India: Portrait of the Aligarh School. In Y. Fehige (ed.), *Science and Religion: East and West.* London: Routledge, 174–188.

Bigliardi, S. (2017a). The "Scientific Miracle of the Qur'ān," Pseudoscience, and Conspiracism. *Zygon, 52*(1), 146–171.

Bigliardi, S. (2017b). Science Refuses to Take Root in Muslim Countries [Interview with P. Hoodbhoy]. *Newsline.* https://newslinemagazine.com/magazine/science-refuses-take-root-muslim-countries-dr-pervez-hoodbhoy/.

Bigliardi, S. (2022). The Unification of the Unifier's Thought and Its Challenges: Abdus Salam's Views on Islam and Science. Essay Review of *Abdus Salam. Une oeuvre entre science et islam* by Ismaël Omarjee,

L'Harmattan, 2021. *Lato Sensu: Revue de la Société de philosophie des sciences*, *9*(1), 28–35. doi: 10.20416/LSRSPS.V9I1.5.

Bojowald, M. (2007). What Happened Before the Big Bang? *Nature Physics*, *3*(8), 523–525.

Bouzenita, A. İ. (2018). "The Most Dangerous Idea?" Islamic Deliberations on Transhumanism. *Darulfunun Ilahiyat*, *29*(2), 201–228.

Bucaille, M. (1976). *La Bible, le Coran et la Science: Les Écritures saintes examinées à la lumière des connaissances modernes*. Paris: Seghers.

Bucaille, M. (1981). *L'homme d'où vient-il? Les réponses de la science et des écritures saintes*. Paris: Seghers.

Burton, E. K. (2010). Teaching Evolution in Muslim States: Iran and Saudi Arabia Compared. *Reports of the National Center for Science Education*, *30*(3), 25–29.

Campanini, M. (2005). Qur'an and Science: A Hermeneutical Approach. *Journal of Qur'anic Studies*, *7*(1), 48–63.

Cheong, P. H. (2020). Robots, Religion and Communication: Rethinking Piety, Practices and Pedagogy in the Era of Artificial Intelligence. In G. Isetti, E. Innerhofer, H. Pechlaner, & M. de Rachewiltz (eds.), *Religion in the Age of Digitalization: From New Media to Spiritual Machines*. London: Routledge, 86–96.

Chittick, W. (2007). *Science of the Cosmos, Science of the Soul: The Pertinence of Islamic Cosmology in the Modern World*. Oxford: Oneworld.

Cho, M. K., & Relman, D. A. (2010). Synthetic "Life," Ethics, National Security, and Public Discourse. *Science*, *329*, 38–39. doi:10.1126/science.1193749.

Clark, K. J., & Koperski, J. (eds.) (2022). *Abrahamic Reflections on Randomness and Providence*. Cham: Palgrave Macmillan.

Clayton, P. (2008). *Adventures in the Spirit: God, World, Divine Action*. Minneapolis, MN: Fortress Press.

Clayton, P., & Railey, M. S. (1998). What Every Teacher of Science and Religion Needs to Know about Pedagogy. *Zygon*, *33*(1), 121–130.

Clément, P. (2015). Muslim Teachers' Conceptions of Evolution in Several Countries. *Public Understanding of Science*, *24*(4), 400–421. doi:10.1177/0963662513494549.

Collins, R. (2016). The Fine-Tuning for Scientific Discovery. In R. Stewart (ed.), *God and Cosmology*. Minneapolis, MN: Fortress Press, 141–168.

Collins, R. (2018). The Argument from Physical Constants: The Fine-Tuning for Discoverability. *Philosophy Educator Scholarship*, *29*. https://mosaic.messiah.edu/phil_ed/29.

Cragg, K. (1998). *Readings in the Qur'an*. Eastbourne: Sussex Academic Press.

Dajani, R. (2015). Why I Teach Evolution to Muslim Students. *Nature*, *520*, 409.

Dallal, A. (2012). Science and Religion in the History of Islam. In D. Marshall (ed.), *Science and Religion: Christian and Muslim Perspectives*. Washington, DC: Georgetown University Press.

Doko, E. (2019). Does Fine-Tuning Need an Explanation? *Kader Kelam Araştırmaları Dergisi*, *17*(1), 1–14.

Draper, P. R. (2005). God, Science, and Naturalism. In W. J. Wainwright (ed.), *The Oxford Handbook of Philosophy of Religion*. Oxford: Oxford University Press, 272–303.

Dyson, F. (2007). *A Many-Colored Glass: Reflections on the Place of Life in the Universe*. Charlottesville, VA: University of Virginia Press.

Edis, T. (2002). *The Ghost in the Universe: God in Light of Modern Science*. Amherst, NY: Prometheus Books.

Edis, T. (2007). *An Illusion of Harmony: Science and Religion in Islam*. Amherst, NY: Prometheus Books.

Edis, T. (2008). *Science and Nonbelief*. Amherst, NY: Prometheus Books.

Edis, T. (2014). On Harmonizing Religion and Science: A Reply to Bigliardi. *Social Epistemology Review and Reply Collective*, *3*(2), 40–43. bit.ly/3uGmSt4.

Edis, T. (2016). *Islam Evolving: Radicalism, Reformation, and the Uneasy Relationship with the Secular West*. Amherst, NY: Prometheus Books.

Ellis, G. F. R. (1995). Ordinary and Extraordinary Divine Action: The Nexus of Interaction. In R. Russell, N. Murphy, & A. Peacocke (eds.), *Chaos and Complexity: Scientific Perspectives on Divine Action*. Vatican: Vatican Observatory, 359–396.

El-Naggar, Z. (2008). *Vérités scientifiques dans le noble Coran*. Beirut: Dar Al-Marefah.

El-Naggar, Z. (2010). *Scientific Precision in the Sunnah: Quotations from the Sayings of Prophet Mohammad (p.b.u.h.)*. Beirut: Dar Al-Marefah.

El-Showk, S. (2016). The Islamic View of the Multiverse. *Nautilus*, December 28. https://nautil.us/the-islamic-view-of-the-multiverse-10157/.

Genç, K. (2018). Turkey's Unnatural Selection: Darwin is the Latest Victim of an Attack on Scientific Values in Turkey's Education System. *Index on Censorship*, *47*(3), 8–10.

Ghaly, M. (2013). Islamic Bioethics in the Twenty-First Century. *Zygon*, *48*(3), 592–599.

Golshani, M. (2000). Islam and the Sciences of Nature: Some Fundamental Questions. *Islamic Studies*, *39*(4), 597–611.

Golshani, M. (2003a). *The Holy Qur'an and the Sciences of Nature: A Theological Reflection*. New York: Global Scholarly Publications.

Golshani, M. (2003b). *Min al-ʿilm al-ʿilmani ila al-ʿilm al-dini* [*From Secular Science to Theistic Science*]. Beirut: Dar Al-Hady.

Golshani, M. (2013). Seek Knowledge Even If It Is in China. *Islam and Science: An Educational Approach*, September 13. https://islam-science.net/seek-knowledge-even-if-it-is-in-china-1260/.

Görke, A. (2010). Die Spaltung des Mondes in der modernen Koranexegese und im Internet. *Welt des Islams, 50*, 60–116.

Guénon, M. (2019). ʿAbd Al-Majīd Al-Zindānī's Iʿjāz ʿIlmī Approach: Embryonic Development in Q. 23: 12–14 as a Scientific Miracle. *Journal of Qurʾanic Studies, 21*(3), 32–56.

Guessoum, N. (2010). *Islam's Quantum Question: Reconciling Muslim Tradition and Modern Science*. London: Bloomsbury Publishing.

Guessoum, N. (2011). [Book review of] *Islam and Biological Evolution: Exploring Classical Sources and Methodologies* by David Solomon Jalajel. *Journal of Islamic Studies, 22*(3), 476–479.

Guessoum, N. (2016a). Islam, Science, Methodological Naturalism, Divine Action, and Miracles. In U. Hasan & A. Osama (eds.), *Islam and Science: Muslim Responses to Science's Big Questions*. www.bit.ly/3VOPoov.

Guessoum, N. (2016b). Islamic Theological views on Darwinian Evolution. In *Oxford Research Encyclopedia of Religion*, May 9. doi: 10.1093/acrefore/9780199340378.013.36.

Guessoum, N. (2018). Science and Religion Issues in Higher Education. In B. Adanan, E. Baydoun, & J. R. Hillman (eds.), *Universities in Arab Countries: An Urgent Need for Change*. Cham: Springer, 187–197.

Guessoum, N. (2022). Randomness in the Cosmos. In K. J. Clark & J. Koperski (eds.), *Abrahamic Reflections on Randomness and Providence*. Cham: Palgrave Macmillan, 57–84.

Hamdy, S. (2008). Rethinking Islamic Legal Ethics in Egypt's Organ Transplant Debate. In J. E. Brockopp & T. Eich (eds.), *Muslim Medical Ethics: From Theory to Practice*. Columbia: University of South Carolina Press, 78–93.

Hejazi, S. (2019). "Humankind. The Best of Molds": Islam Confronting Transhumanism. *Sophia, 58*(4), 677–688. doi:10.1007/s11841-019-00755-7.

Hoodbhoy, P. (1991). *Islam and Science: Religious Orthodoxy and the Battle for Rationality*. London: Zed Books.

Hoodbhoy, P. (2015). An Exchange on Science and the Supernatural in Pakistani Universities. *Social Epistemology Review and Reply Collective*, November 2. bit.ly/3Q6yhMS

Howard, D. (2011). *Being Human in Islam: The Impact of the Evolutionary Worldview*. London: Routledge.

Iqbal, M. (2007). *Science and Islam*. Westport, CT: Greenwood Press.

Jalajel, D. S. (2009). *Islam and Biological Evolution: Exploring Classical Sources and Methodologies*. Bellville: University of the Western Cape.

Jalajel, D. S. (2018). *Tawaqquf and Acceptance of Human Evolution*. Irving, TX: Yaqeen Institute publications. https://bit.ly/3icdrPp.

Karapehlivan, F. (2019). Constructing a "New Turkey" through Education: An Overview of the Education Policies in Turkey under the AKP Rule. *Heinrich Böll Stiftung*, October 1. https://bit.ly/3IiRPMe.

Khan, N., and Qadhi, Y. (2018). *Human Origins: Theological Conclusions and Empirical Limitations*. Irving, TX: Yaqeen Institute Publications. https://bit .ly/3VNh8sU.

Khokhar, M. S. (2018). Fine Tuning and the Holy Qur'an. *Advanced Humanities and Social Sciences*, *3*, 37–38.

Kirmani, M. Z. (2015). The Aligarh School of Islam and Science Studies: Understanding Its Background and Distinctive Features. *Social Epistemology Review and Reply Collective*, *4*(10), 33–46. https://social-epis temology.com/2015/10/23/the-aligarh-school-of-islam-and-science-studies-understanding-its-background-and-distinctive-features-m-zaki-kirmani/

Kurniawan, B. (n.d.). Islamizing Social Science: The Politics of Islamization of Science on Several Higher Education Institutions in Indonesia. https://bit.ly/ 3X1xIpY.

Lewis, G. F., and Barnes, L. A. (2016). *A Fortunate Universe: Life in a Finely Tuned Cosmos*. Cambridge, UK: Cambridge University Press.

Malik, S. (2020). Islam and Evolution: The Curious Case of David Solomon Jalajel. In S. A. Schleifer (ed.), *The Muslim 500: The World's 500 Most Influential Muslims, 2021*. Amman: The Royal Islamic Strategic Studies Centre, 251–254.

Mansour, N. (2019). Science, Religion, and Pedagogy: Teachers' Issues. In B. Billingsley, K. Chappell, & M. J. Reiss (eds.), *Science and Religion in Education*. Cham: Springer, 315–336.

Matthews, Z. (2021). A Review of the Rulings by Muslim Jurists on Assisted Reproductive Technology and Reproductive Tissue Transplantation. *Religions*, *12*(9), 720–730. doi: 10.3390/rel12090720

Mavani, H. (2014). God's Deputy: Islam and Transhumanism. In C. Mercer & D. F. Maher (eds.), *Transhumanism and the Body: The World Religions Speak*. Cham: Palgrave Macmillan, 67–84.

Mimouni, J. (2015). Should Religion Be Kept Out of the Science Classroom? In N. Guessoum & A. Osama (eds.), *Science at the Universities of the Muslim World*, 83–86: http://muslim-science.com/wp-content/uploads/2015/11/ Science_at_Universities_of_the_Muslim_World.pdf.

Moore, K. L. (1983). *The Developing Human, Clinically Oriented Embryology with Islamic Additions, Correralations [sic] Studies with Qur'an and Hadith*

(*A. M. A. Azzindani*), 3rd ed. Jeddah: Dar Al-Qiblah for Islamic Literature. www.tinyurl.com/2p83ex9s.

Muğaloğlu, E. Z. (2018). An Insight into Evolution Education in Turkey. In H. Deniz & L. Borgerding (eds.), *Evolution Education Around the Globe.* Cham: Springer, 263–279.

Mujahed, M. (2004). *Usus al-manhaj al-Qur'ani fi bahth al-'ulum al-tabi'iyya* [*The Bases of the Qur'anic Methodology in the Study of the Natural Sciences*], 2nd ed. Jeddah: Ad-Dar As-Su'udiyya li-l-Nashr wa-l-Tawzi'a.

Mutahhari, M. (1922). *Farizeh 'Ilm* [*The Duty of Knowledge*]. Tehran: Goftar-e Mah.

Nasr, S. H. (1964). *An Introduction to Islamic Cosmological Doctrines: Conceptions of Nature and Methods Used for Its Study by the Ikhwān Al-safā', Al-Bīrunī and Ibn Sīnā.* Cambridge, MA: Belknap Press of Harvard University Press.

Nasr, S. H. (1981). *Knowledge and the Sacred: The Gifford Lectures, 1981.* Edinburgh: Edinburgh University Press.

Nasr, S. H. (1982). Islam and Modern Science. In S. Azzam (ed.), *Islam and Contemporary Society.* London: Addison-Wesley Longman, 177–190.

Nasr, S. H. (1993). *The Need for a Sacred Science.* London: Curzon.

Nasr, S. H., & Iqbal, M. (2007). *Islam, Science, Muslims and Technology: Seyyed Hossein Nasr in Conversation with Muzaffar Iqbal.* Sherwood Park, AB: Al-Qalam Publishing.

Okasha, S. (2016). *Philosophy of Science: A Very Short Introduction.* Oxford: Oxford University Press.

Omarjee, I. (2021). *Abdus Salam: Une œuvre entre science et Islam.* Paris: L'Harmattan.

Padela, A. I. (ed.). (2021) *Medicine and Shariah: A Dialogue in Islamic Bioethics.* Notre Dame, IN: University of Notre Dame Press.

Parray, T. A. (2015). Sir Sayyid Ahmad Khan (1817–1898) on Taqlid, Ijtihad, and Science-Religion Compatibility. *Social Epistemology Review and Reply Collective, 4*(6), 19–34. https://tinyurl.com/4znre2tv

Peker, D., Comert, G. G., & Kence, A. (2010). Three Decades of Anti-Evolution Campaign and Its Results: Turkish Undergraduates' Acceptance and Understanding of the Biological Evolution Theory. *Science & Education, 19*, 739–755.

Piraino, F. (2014). Bruno Guiderdoni – among Sufism, Traditionalism and Science: A Reply to Bigliardi. *Social Epistemology Review and Reply Collective, 3* (11), 21–24: https://tinyurl.com/5ebskstu.

Rady, M. Y., and Verheijde, J. L. (2009). Islam and End-of-Life Organ Donation: Asking the Right Questions. *Saudi Medical Journal, 30*(7), 882–886.

Raquib, A., Channa, B., Zubair, T. et al. (2022). Islamic Virtue-Based Ethics for Artificial Intelligence. *Discover Artificial Intelligence*, 2, 11.

Reed, R. (2021). AI in Religion, AI for Religion, AI and Religion: Towards a Theory of Religious Studies and Artificial Intelligence. *Religions*, *12*(6), 401. www.mdpi.com/2077-1444/12/6/401/htm.

Renan, E. (1862). *De la part des peuples sémitiques dans l'histoire de la civilisation : discours d'ouverture du cours de langues hébraïque, chaldaïque et syriaque, au Collège de France*. Available as ebook from the Bibliothèque Nationale de France: https://gallica.bnf.fr/ark:/12148/bpt6k29776q/f1.item.

Riexinger, M. (2009). Abdus Salam: A Nobel Physicist from the Muslim World. In N. A. Rupke (ed.), *Eminent Lives in Twentieth-Century Science & Religion*. 2nd revised and much expanded ed. Frankfurt am Main: Peter Lang, 317–332.

Ross Solberg, A. (2013). *The Mahdi Wears Armani: An Analysis of the Harun Yahya Enterprise*, Huddinge: Södertörn University Press.

Rustom, M. (2017). The Great Chain of Consciousness. *Renovatio*, April 28. https://renovatio.zaytuna.edu/article/the-great-chain-of-consciousness.

Salam, A. (1984). Islam and Science. In C. H. Lai (ed.), *Ideals and Realities. Selected Essays of Abdus Salam* (2nd ed. published 1987). Singapore: World Scientific, 179–213.

Salam, A. (1986). The Future of Science in Islamic Countries. In C. H. Lai (ed.), *Ideals and Realities: Selected Essays of Abdus Salam* (2nd ed. published 1987). Singapore: World Scientific, 214–240.

Salam, A. (1991). Foreword. In P. Hoodbhoy, *Islam and Science. Religious Orthodoxy and the Battle for Rationality*. London: Zed Books, ix–xi. (Foreword written in 1990)

Sardar, Z. (ed.). (1984). *The Touch of Midas: Science, Values, and Environment in Islam and the West*. Manchester: Manchester University Press.

Sardar, Z. (1985). Between Two Masters: Qur'an or Science? *Inquiry: Critical Thinking Across the Disciplines*, *2*(8), 37–41.

Sardar, Z. (1989). *Explorations in Islamic Science*. London: Mansell.

Sardar, Z. (2004). *Desperately Seeking Paradise: Journeys of a Sceptical Muslim*. London: Granta Books.

Sardar, Z. (2006a). Muslims and Philosophy of Science. In E. Masood (ed.), *How Do You Know?* London: Pluto, 108–113.

Sardar, Z. (2006b). Islamic Science: The Way Ahead. In E. Masood (ed.), *How Do You Know?* London: Pluto, 161–192.

Saunders, N. (2002). *Divine Action and Modern Science*. Cambridge, UK: Cambridge University Press.

Sedgwick, M. (2004). *Against the Modern World: Traditionalism and the Secret Intellectual History of the Twentieth Century.* Oxford: Oxford University Press.

Setia, A. (2003). Al-Attas' Philosophy of Science: An Extended Outline. *Islam & Science, 1*(2), 165–214.

Singler, B. (2017). An Introduction to Artificial Intelligence and Religion for the Religious Studies Scholar. *Implicit Religion, 20*(3), 215–231.

Ssekamanya, S.A., Suhailah, H., and Nik Ahmad, H. I. (2011). The Experience of Islamization of Knowledge at the International Islamic University Malaysia: Successes and Challenges. *New Intellectual Horizons in Education*, 91–110.

Stenberg, L. (1996). *The Islamization of Science: Four Muslim Positions Developing an Islamic Modernity.* Lund: Religionshistoriska avdelningen, Lunds universitet.

Taji-Farouki, S. (2004). Introduction. In S. Taji-Farouki (ed.), *Modern Muslim Intellectuals and the Qur'an* London: Oxford University Press, 1–36.

Tarhan, N. (2012). Consciousness. In *Questions on Islam.* https://questionsonislam .com/article/consciousness.

Taslaman, C. (2022). Can a Muslim Be an Evolutionist? In K. J. Clark & J. Koperski (eds.), *Abrahamic Reflections on Randomness and Providence.* Cham: Palgrave Macmillan, 107–117.

Tee, C. (2016). *The Gülen Movement in Turkey: The Politics of Islam and Modernity.* London and New York: I. B. Tauris.

Vauthier, J. (1990). *Abdus Salam un physicien: Entretien avec Jacques Vauthier.* Paris: Beauchesne.

Wiles, M. (1999). *Reason to Believe.* London: SCM Press.

Woodman, A., Al-Bar, M. A, & Chamsi-Pasha, H. (2019). Introduction to Islamic Medical Ethics. *Journal of the British Islamic Medical Association, 2*(1), 1–5.

Yazicioglu, U. I. (2013). *Understanding the Qur'anic Miracle Stories in the Modern Age.* University Park, PA: Pennsylvania State University Press.

Ziadat, A. A. (1986). *Western Science in the Arab World: The Impact of Darwinism, 1860–1930.* London: MacMillan.

Acknowledgments

We wish to thank Alex Wright and the staff at Cambridge University Press for having entrusted us with both the Elements series on Islam and the sciences and this overview booklet, which we hope will help widen interest in the subject and entice many to pick up some of its varied topics. We also wish to thank numerous colleagues who have helped us by pointing to useful references.

We acknowledge funds from the Sheikha Nama Majid Al Qassimi Endowed Chair in Education Across Disciplines that Nidhal Guessoum holds at the American University of Sharjah, UAE.

And last but not least, we wish to thank the reviewers for their constructive comments, which helped improve the contents and clarity of this Element.

Cambridge Elements

Islam and the Sciences

Nidhal Guessoum

American University of Sharjah, United Arab Emirates

Nidhal Guessoum is Professor of Astrophysics at the American University of Sharjah, United Arab Emirates. Besides Astrophysics, he has made notable contributions in Science & Islam/Religion, education, and the public understanding of science; he has published books on these subjects in several languages, including *The Story of the Universe* (in Arabic, first edition in 1997), *Islam's Quantum Question* (in English in 2010, translated into several languages), and *The Young Muslim's Guide to Modern Science* (in English 2019, translated into several languages), numerous articles (academic and popular science), and vast social-media activity.

Stefano Bigliardi

Al Akhawayn University in Ifrane, Morocco

Stefano Bigliardi is Associate Professor of Philosophy at Al Akhawayn University in Ifrane, Morocco. He trained as a philosopher of science, has a PhD in philosophy from the University of Bologna, and has served in different positions at universities in Germany, Sweden, Mexico, and Switzerland. He has published a monograph and a popular science book on Islam and Science as well as dozens of articles (peer-reviewed and popular) on the subject and others. Since 2016, he has taught undergraduate courses on Islam and Science at Al Akhawayn University in Ifrane, Morocco.

About the Series

Elements in Islam and the Sciences is a new platform for the exploration, critical review and concise analysis of Islamic engagements with the sciences: past, present and future. The series will not only assess ideas, arguments and positions; it will also present novel views that push forward the frontiers of the field. These Elements will evince strong philosophical, theological, historical, and social dimensions as they address interactions between Islam and a wide range of scientific subjects.

Cambridge Elements ☰

Islam and the Sciences

Elements in the Series

Islam and Science: Past, Present, and Future Debates
Nidhal Guessoum and Stefano Bigliardi

A full series listing is available at: www.cambridge.org/EISC

Printed in the United States
by Baker & Taylor Publisher Services